dBASE IV®

Sarah E. Hutchinson
Stacey C. Sawyer
Glen J. Coulthard

THE IRWIN ADVANTAGE SERIES
FOR COMPUTER EDUCATION

IRWIN
Burr Ridge, Illinois
Boston, Massachusetts
Sydney, Australia

©Richard D. Irwin, Inc., 1993

Printed in the United States of America.

ISBN 0-256-13518-5

dBase IV is a registered trademark of Borland International.

5 6 7 8 9 0 ML 0 9 8 7 6 5 4 3

CONTENTS

SESSION 2
MANAGING AND ORGANIZING DATA WITH dBASE IV   49

SESSION 3
QUERIES   73

SESSION 4
CREATING FORMS, REPORTS, AND LABELS   109

SESSION 5
MANAGING FILES AND ADVANCED TOPICS   141

USING THIS GUIDE

This tutorial is one in a series of learning guides that lead you through the most popular microcomputer software programs available. Concepts, skills, and procedures are grouped into session topics and are presented in a logical and structured manner. Commands and procedures are introduced using hands-on examples, and you are encouraged to perform the steps along with the guide. Although you may turn directly to a later session, be aware that some sessions require, or at least assume, that you have completed the previous sessions. For maximum benefit, you should work through the short-answer and hands-on exercises appearing at the end of each session.

The exercises and examples in this guide use several standard conventions to indicate menu keystroke combinations and command instructions.

KEYSTROKES AND KEYSTROKE COMBINATIONS

When you must press two keys together, the tutorial's instruction line shows the keys joined with a plus sign (+). For example, to include a field in a label form, you must hold down **Ctrl** and then press **End**. The following line illustrates this type of keystroke combination:

PRESS: **Ctrl**+**End**

This instruction tells you to press **Ctrl** first and then hold it down while you press **End**. Once both keys have been pressed, they are then immediately released.

COMMAND INSTRUCTIONS

This guide indicates with a special typeface data that you are required to type in yourself. For example:

TYPE: George Washington

When you are required to enter unique information, such as the current date or your name, the instructions appear in *italics*. The following instruction directs you to type your name in place of the actual words: "your name."

TYPE: *your name*

THE FUNDAMENTALS OF dBASE IV

Modern database management systems for microcomputers provide the business user with the means of managing and manipulating large amounts of data. They were introduced to the business community for use on microcomputers at about the same time as electronic spreadsheets. Received with great enthusiasm, both types of software packages are powerful and easy to use, and they are often used together. This session introduces you to the fundamentals of using the popular database management systems (DBMS) package named dBASE IV.

PREVIEW

When you have completed this session, you will be able to:

Describe what a database management system is.
•
Describe DBMS features that are important to know about when you are:
Creating and adding data.
Searching a database.
Reordering a database.
Modifying a database's structure.
Creating and printing reports.
•
Use dBASE IV to create a database and add data.
•
Modify the database structure.
•
Save and use a database.
•
Add records to a database.
•
Display and edit database records.
•
Print a list of database records.

1

SESSION OUTLINE

WHY IS THIS SESSION IMPORTANT?

Picture an office with a row of file cabinets that extends as far as you can see—and you're responsible for them! You use your filing system mainly to track customer-related information, and everything is perfectly organized in alphabetical order by last name. Not even one customer name is out of place! You know exactly where to look to find information on each customer. Great. But what if you need to pull out all folders that contain information on customers who live in a particular area? Your alphabetical organization scheme would no longer be useful. Your manual filing system has become a problem. You need a microcomputer database management system! A **database management system (DBMS)** is a software tool that facilitates creating and maintaining an information database and producing reports from it. The term **database** describes a collection of data stored for a variety of business purposes.

Let's look at another example. You are a salesperson whose territory covers Indiana and Ohio. You have over a hundred clients to keep track of and are thinking of using a computer-based database management system to keep track of the data. Once you have entered all the data pertaining to each client into your computer, then for only the cost of keeping the data current, you have a very valuable tool at your fingertips. You're making a trip through northern Ohio? In a few minutes, you can produce a report showing all the customers in that area prioritized by annual sales and the date of the most recent sales call. You can't remember why a client wasn't interested in your product during the last visit? In a few seconds, you can display on your screen any memo text that pertains to that client.

This session explains the features of a microcomputer-based DBMS and teaches you the fundamentals of using dBASE IV to create, add data to, display, and edit the data stored in a database.

Before proceeding, make sure the following are true:

1. You have access to dBASE IV.

2. Your Advantage Diskette is inserted in the drive. You will save your work onto the diskette and retrieve the files that have been created for you. (*Note*: The Advantage Diskette can be made by copying all the files off the instructor's Master Advantage Diskette onto a formatted diskette.)

DBMS FEATURES

As with any software package, you must be familiar with the concepts and features of a DBMS before you can start to use it. This section introduces you to these concepts and features so that when you begin using dBASE IV later in this session, you will understand the whys and whats of DBMS processing.

It is important that you understand a few terms before creating a database and using database software. To define these terms we will use the analogy of a filing cabinet:

- *File*. Think of a database file as analogous to a filing cabinet. In this filing cabinet you might store information for each of your employees in folders.

- *Record*. Think of a record as analogous to a folder in a filing cabinet. Each folder, or record, should contain the same type of data. For example, when storing employee information, each folder would include name, address, phone, and salary data.

- *Field*. Think of a field as analogous to an individual piece of information in a folder, such as a name or address. When creating a database structure, you must define the characteristics of the fields that you want to include in each database record.

CREATING A DATABASE

After you have loaded dBASE IV into RAM, you can begin using its commands to create or manage a database. Creating a database is often referred to as creating the **database structure**—defining exactly what you want each field in a database record to look like. Think of this activity as defining what kind of information each folder should contain. (For example, in a client database, do you want to keep track of the client's name and business address? phone number? names of products purchased? value of product purchases? and so on.)

Figure 1.1 shows a database file structure that was defined using dBASE IV. This file structure was saved onto a data disk under the name of EMPLOYEE. To create a structure using dBASE IV, the following items must be defined:

Figure 1.1

Database structure for the EMPLOYEE database

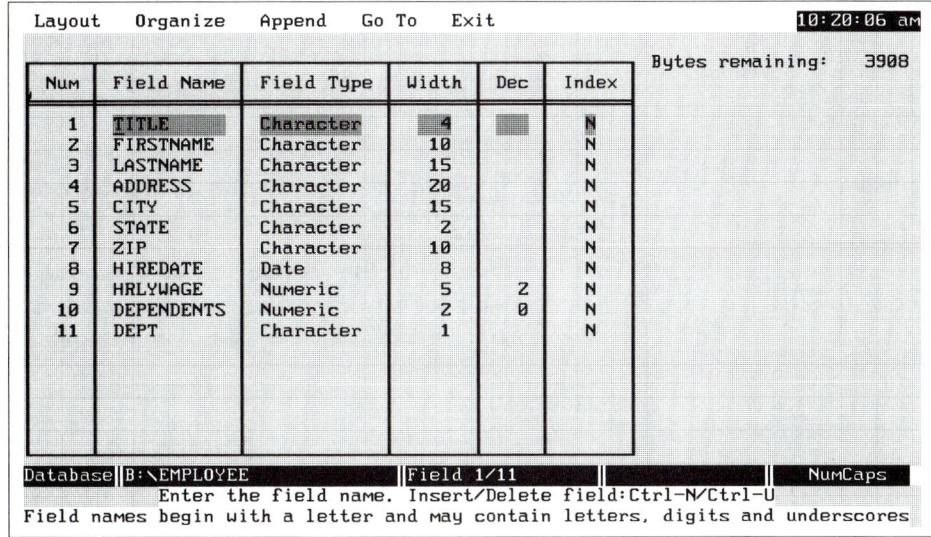

```
  Layout   Organize   Append   Go To   Exit                    10:20:06 am

                                                    Bytes remaining:   3908

  ┌─────┬────────────┬────────────┬───────┬─────┬───────┐
  │ Num │ Field Name │ Field Type │ Width │ Dec │ Index │
  ├─────┼────────────┼────────────┼───────┼─────┼───────┤
  │  1  │ TITLE      │ Character  │   4   │     │   N   │
  │  2  │ FIRSTNAME  │ Character  │  10   │     │   N   │
  │  3  │ LASTNAME   │ Character  │  15   │     │   N   │
  │  4  │ ADDRESS    │ Character  │  20   │     │   N   │
  │  5  │ CITY       │ Character  │  15   │     │   N   │
  │  6  │ STATE      │ Character  │   2   │     │   N   │
  │  7  │ ZIP        │ Character  │  10   │     │   N   │
  │  8  │ HIREDATE   │ Date       │   8   │     │   N   │
  │  9  │ HRLYWAGE   │ Numeric    │   5   │  2  │   N   │
  │ 10  │ DEPENDENTS │ Numeric    │   2   │  0  │   N   │
  │ 11  │ DEPT       │ Character  │   1   │     │   N   │
  └─────┴────────────┴────────────┴───────┴─────┴───────┘

  Database B:\EMPLOYEE                   Field 1/11              NumCaps
             Enter the field name. Insert/Delete field:Ctrl-N/Ctrl-U
  Field names begin with a letter and may contain letters, digits and underscores
```

1. *Field name.* You must give a unique name to each field of data you want to store. A **field name** can be no longer than 10 characters. To manipulate the database, you will often be required to refer to one or more elements of data by their field names. Although field names must begin with a letter, you can use letters, numbers, and underscores when naming fields. Blank spaces aren't allowed in field names, nor any other punctuation marks or special characters.

2. *Field type.* DBMS programs require you to define what type of information will be stored in the field; in other words, you must define the **field type**. With dBASE IV, data can be one of six types: (a) **character**—data that is **nonnumeric**, such as name and address information; (b) **numeric**—data that will be used in calculations, such as dollar amounts; (c) **float**—data stored as a *floating point* number (typically used in scientific applications) speed up operations that require extensive multiplying and dividing of very large and very small numbers; (d) **date**—data that must be entered in a specific date format so that calculations can be performed on it; (e) **logical**—data that indicates whether a field is true or false (such as data regarding a person's marital status, where true = married and false = single); and (f) **memo**—data in the form of a long paragraph of text.

3. *Field width.* You must determine what the maximum size of the field will be—its **field width**. For example, if you are defining the structure for a field that is to contain an employee's last name, what is the longest name you will probably have? Will it be 10, 20, or 30 characters long?

You must be sure that enough space is available for all the data you want to enter. You don't have to enter field widths for date (8 positions wide), logical (1 position wide), or memo fields (10 positions wide). The widths for these are set automatically by dBASE IV.

4. *Decimal places.* For each numeric field, you must determine the number of decimal places you want. Users often store numbers to two decimal places (such as $10.00) instead of no decimal places (such as $10). The number of decimal places that you assign to the width of a numeric or floating point field must be at least two less than the width of the field. The decimal places and decimal point take up space in a field.

5. *Index.* When creating the structure for a database, you can also specify that once you add data to the database, you want it to be displayed in order by a particular field. You can accomplish this by creating an **index file** that will put the database into order. Indexing is described in more detail in Session 2.

You must think carefully about these definitions at the start so you won't have to change your database structure later, after you've entered a number of different records. It is possible to modify a database structure, but depending on the changes you make, you may lose data. (Modifying a database structure is described in more detail shortly.) Before the EMPLOYEE database file structure was created, for example, thought was given to having a separate field for TITLE, FIRSTNAME, and LASTNAME because (1) the database can now be sorted into alphabetical order by last name, and (2) the individual name fields can be referenced in a report. For example, you might want to include only TITLE (Mr., Ms., Miss, or Mrs.) and LASTNAME fields in a specific report. When designing the structure for a database, a good rule of thumb is to give every individual piece of data its own field. Otherwise it is sometimes difficult to search for or access the data you want to work with.

ADDING DATA TO A DATABASE

Once you have defined your database structure, you can add data to it. However, because you will often have more than one database file stored on the same disk, first you must tell dBASE IV to which file you want to add data. We lead you through adding new records to a database file later in this session. Figure 1.2 pictures a listing of the database file called EMPLOYEE (the structure for this database is pictured in Figure 1.1) after 12 records have been entered.

Figure 1.2

EMPLOYEE
database file.
These records
were keyed into
the structure
shown in
Figure 1.1.

```
Record#  TITLE  FIRSTNAME  LASTNAME    ADDRESS
    1    Mr.    Rod        Bannister   7279 Ridge Drive
    2    Ms.    Evelyn     Chabot      2613 Henderson Hiway
    3    Mr.    Ahmad      Arguello    4 Chestnut Lane
    4    Mr.    Michael    Antonucci   4901 101st Place SW
    5    Ms.    Rosalie    Gills       1350 Beverly Road
    6    Mr.    Bradley    Wachowiak   700 Cumberland Court
    7    Ms.    Karen      Shepherd    3107 Peachtree Drive
    8    Ms.    Kathleen   Salazar     75 Dorado Terrace
    9    Mr.    Arthur     Sotak       1217 Carlisle Road
   10    Ms.    Jean       Hurtado     3202 E Dry Creek Rd
   11    Mr.    Robert     Keller      416 Whittier Drive
   12    Mr.    Herbert    Licon       1220 E Barcelona
```

```
Record#  CITY           STATE  ZIP     HIREDATE   HRLYWAGE  DEPENDENTS  DEPT
    1    San Mateo      CA     94001   05/06/91   17.00          2       A
    2    San Diego      CA     95609   02/14/91   18.00          1       B
    3    San Mateo      CA     94001   01/04/91   19.00          0       A
    4    San Francisco  CA     94104   01/05/91   11.00          3       B
    5    San Francisco  CA     94109   03/16/91   21.00          0       B
    6    San Mateo      CA     94001   05/11/91   19.50          2       A
    7    San Mateo      CA     94001   02/06/90   21.00          0       A
    8    San Francisco  CA     94104   11/13/90   16.50          2       B
    9    San Mateo      CA     94001   11/04/90   23.00          0       A
   10    San Diego      CA     95609   11/04/90   10.50          1       B
   11    San Francisco  CA     94109   01/03/90   17.00          4       A
   12    San Francisco  CA     94001   09/01/91   17.00          0       A
```

SEARCHING A DATABASE

What if you want to see a list—either on your screen or printed out—of only those elements of your database that meet certain criteria? In a manual file system, depending on how the folders are organized, you might need a long time to perform special searches to respond to requests such as: "Pull out the folders in the employee filing cabinet for every employee who makes more than $15.00 per hour." If the folders are organized in alphabetical order by name, this could take hours! In contrast, performing **searches** with DBMS software and database files stored in computer-usable form is fast and, once you get comfortable with the procedure, easy. As long as you know the field names defined in your database structure (such as TITLE and FIRSTNAME) and are familiar with the types of operations you can perform, you can ask the DBMS for the answer to any number of questions about your database. In Session 3, you will practice searching your database for specific information.

There are five categories of database management operations: (1) arithmetic operations, (2) relational operations, (3) logical operations, (4) sound searches, and (5) pattern searches.

- *Arithmetic operations.* You can perform **arithmetic operations** on the numeric fields in your database. The arithmetic operators are:
    + Addition
    - Subtraction
    * Multiplication
    / Division
    ( ) Parentheses are used for grouping operations

- *Relational operations.* **Relational operations** are used to analyze the contents of fields. For example, you would need to use a relational operator if you want to list the records in your EMPLOYEE database file that have an hourly wage field that contains an amount greater than 15 (Figure 1.3), to list all employees who work in Department A (Figure 1.4).

Figure 1.3

Listing those records in the EMPLOYEE database that have an hourly wage amount that is greater than 15. The relational operation used was HRLYWAGE>15.

Records	Organize	Fields	Go To	Exit		
TITLE	FIRSTNAME	LASTNAME	CITY		HRLYWAGE	DEPT
Mr.	Rod	Bannister	San Mateo		17.00	A
Ms.	Evelyn	Chabot	San Diego		18.00	B
Mr.	Ahmad	Arguello	San Mateo		19.00	A
Ms.	Rosalie	Gills	San Francisco		21.00	B
Mr.	Bradley	Wachowiak	San Mateo		19.50	A
Ms.	Karen	Shepherd	San Mateo		21.00	A
Ms.	Kathleen	Salazar	San Francisco		16.50	B
Mr.	Arthur	Sotak	San Mateo		23.00	A
Mr.	Robert	Keller	San Francisco		17.00	A
Mr.	Herbert	Licon	San Francisco		17.00	A

Browse	B:\<NEW>	Rec 1/12	View		Num

Figure 1.4

Listing those employees who work in Department A. The relational operation used was DEPT="A".

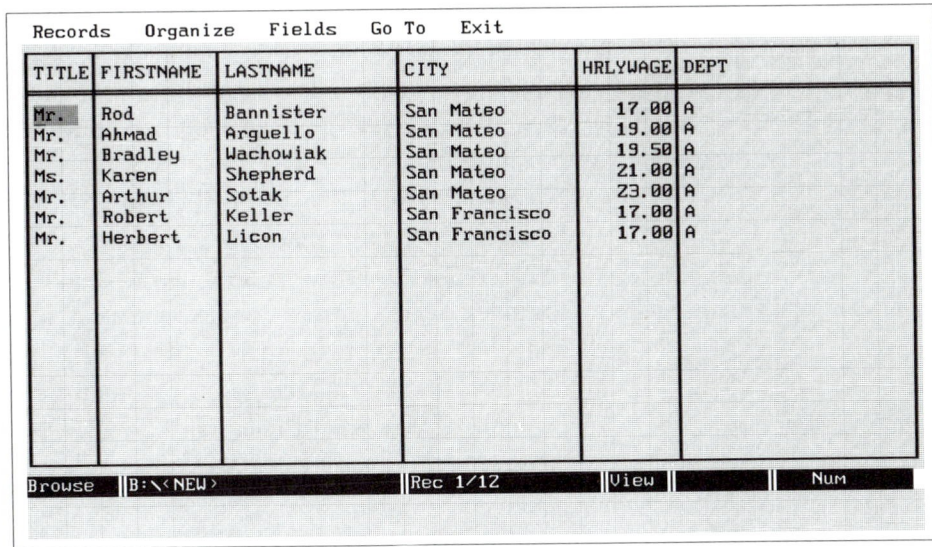

With dBASE IV, the following relational operators can be used:

> Greater than
< Less than
= Equal to
>= Greater than or equal to
<= Less than or equal to
<> Not equal to

The result of relational operations is always a true (T) or a false (F) answer. Another operation is usually performed on the basis of the answer, such as listing the record on the screen.

- *Logical operations.* **Logical operations** allow you to search your database for special information. For example, you might want to list on the screen all the employees who earn more than $15 per hour *and* who work in San Diego. Two commonly used logical operators are described below; each begins and ends with a period (.):

.AND.   Allows you to specify that two or more conditions exist before a specific action is taken. For example, using the EMPLOYEE database, test to determine if CITY = San Francisco *and* ZIP = 94104. This command would allow you to screen out all employees except those who live in San Francisco's 94104 ZIP code area.

.OR. Allows you to specify that at least one condition must exist before a specific action is taken. For example, test to determine if CITY = San Francisco *or* CITY = San Mateo. This command would allow you to screen out all employees except those who live in San Francisco or San Mateo.

- *Sound searches.* The *Sounds-like* operator is used to search for a word in a database that you aren't sure how to spell. However you think you know how it sounds. A mathematical code, called the Soundex code, is used to describe how a particular word sounds and then attempt to match that sound to other words in the database that sound the same but may be spelled differently. For example, if you want to search the FIRSTNAME field for Sarah or Sara, you could search for *Sounds like "sara."*

- *Pattern searches.* The *Like* operator can be used to search for a particular string of characters in a field. The asterisk (*) and question mark (?) can be used as wildcard characters. For example, to search for all records that include "95" as the first two characters in the ZIP field, you would search for 95*.

REORDERING A DATABASE

When you ask a DBMS to list, or search for, specific records based on certain criteria, the list displays the record data in the order you input it to the database file. How, then, can you list records in chronological order (by date), for example? You can either sort or index a database into order. Note that these two commands offer very different ways to access the data in a file in a particular sequence. As described in Session 2, indexing files into a particular order is generally preferable to sorting files into order.

MODIFYING A DATABASE'S STRUCTURE

What happens if, after you've entered hundreds of records, you realize you need to modify the structure of your database? Perhaps you want to add a field to each record in the EMPLOYEE database—for example, employee number (EMPNUM). In the early days of DBMS software, this procedure would have been difficult. Recent versions of DBMS software make the problem easier to deal with; however, certain database changes are more difficult to accomplish than others.

One of the most common structure changes that users make affects field width—sufficient space was not allotted initially. As you will see later in this session, changing the field width is easy. However, changing the type of the field—for example, from character to numeric—can cause you to lose data.

CREATING AND PRINTING REPORTS

You've learned that you can manipulate a database by sorting, indexing, and/or listing records that meet your specifications or criteria. Frequently you will want the results of these manipulations to be output in a polished form that can be circulated throughout your company for review. Fortunately, database software provides you with the capability to output the results of your processing activities to a report. This report might include totals and subtotals, arithmetic (based on the numeric fields in your database), and stylized headings and subheadings.

For instance, you may want to include in a report for the company's executives (using data from the EMPLOYEE database) a listing containing LASTNAME, FIRSTNAME, HIREDATE, and HRLYWAGE fields for all the employees who work in Department A. Without using the report session—using only a simple LIST command—the listing looks something like Figure 1.4. But if you use dBASE's reporting commands, the listing might look like Figure 1.5.

Figure 1.5

Using the CREATE REPORT command to list database records

```
Page No.    1
01/14/93

         FIRST    LAST                         HOURLY
TITLE    FIRST    NAME          CITY            WAGE      DEPARTMENT

Mr.      Rod      Bannister     San Mateo       17.00     A
Mr.      Ahmad    Arguello      San Mateo       19.00     A
Mr.      Bradley  Wachowiak     San Mateo       19.50     A
Ms.      Karen    Shepherd      San Mateo       21.00     A
Mr.      Arthur   Sotak         San Mateo       23.00     A
Mr.      Robert   Keller        San Francisco   17.00     A
Mr.      Herbert  Licon         San Francisco   17.00     A
                                                133.50




          Cancel viewing: ESC.  Continue viewing: SPACEBAR
```

LOADING DBASE IV

Because the dBASE IV package contains so many program instructions, your computer must be configured with a hard disk for you to run it. In other words, you cannot load dBASE from diskettes—dBASE must be loaded from the hard disk. (As mentioned earlier, you will, however, store the files you create on your Advantage Diskette.)

To load dBASE IV into RAM, perform the following steps:

1. dBASE IV is probably loaded in a subdirectory (named something like DBASE) on the hard disk. You may be able to load dBASE IV without making the dBASE subdirectory the current directory. To see if this is the case, type the following after the system prompt:
   TYPE: dbase
   PRESS: Enter
   If a message such as "Bad Command or Filename" is displaying on the screen, proceed with steps 2–3. Otherwise, skip steps 2–3.

2. Use the CD command to make the dBASE subdirectory the current subdirectory. For example, if the dBASE subdirectory is called DBASE, you would type CD \DBASE and then press Enter to accomplish this. (Ask your instructor or lab assistant what the name of the subdirectory is.)

3. To load dBASE IV:
   TYPE: dbase
   PRESS: Enter

4. A brief copyright message should now be displaying on the screen. After a few seconds, the screen will automatically change to display the Control Center (Figure 1.6).

THE CONTROL CENTER

The **Control Center** is the center of the dBASE IV menu system. You must become familiar with it before performing any database activities.

Figure 1.6

The Control
Center. This is
what you see
(after the copy-
right message)
when dBASE IV
is first loaded
into RAM.

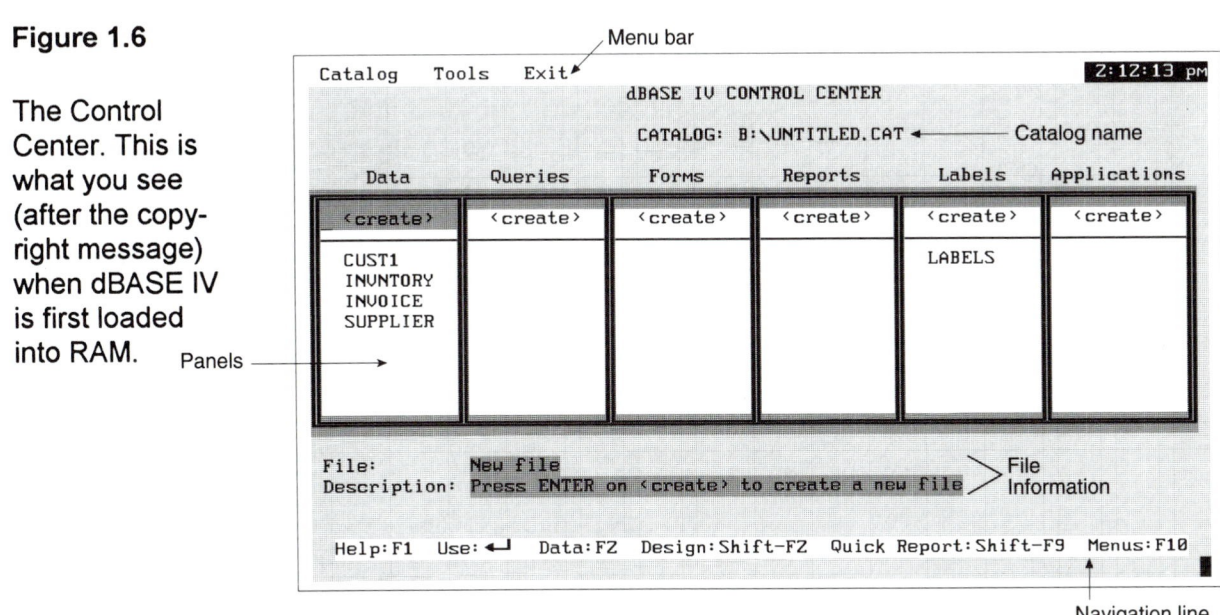

As shown in Figure 1.6, the Control Center is composed of the following:

- *Menu bar*. The menu bar is displaying at the very top of the screen. It contains the following three menu options:

  - *Catalog menu*. This menu provides you with options to create or modify a **catalog**, which is a means by which you can group related database files. For example, you would want to group two databases together if you frequently need to retrieve information from them at the same time. Catalogs are described in more detail at the end of this session.

  - *Tools menu*. This menu provides file management options and options for modifying the appearance of the screen. This menu is described in Session 5.

  - *Exit menu*. This menu provides options for exiting to (1) the dot prompt, which displays when you exit the Control Center (the dot prompt is described in the next section) or (2) the DOS prompt, which displays when you exit dBASE.

- *Catalog name*. If you create a catalog name, its name will display near the top of the screen.

- *Panels.* The **panels** in the Control Center are the six vertical sections that make up most of the screen. Each panel enables you to create a different type of file that provides you with specific capabilities. The **<create> marker** in each panel is used to create the file, giving you a different dBASE screen for each panel chosen. You can create the following types of files:

  - Choose the Data panel to create database files. You learn how to create a database file in this session.

  - Choose the Queries panel to create files that are used to retrieve information from or update a database (Session 3).

  - Choose the Forms panel to create files that contain your data entry form specifications (Session 4). (These files typically make it easier to work with a database because your screen interface with the database is customized to your particular needs.)

  - Choose the Reports panel to create files that contain your specifications for stylized reports and for form letters (Session 4).

  - Choose the Labels panel to create files that contain mailing label specifications (Session 4).

  - Choose the Applications panel to create program files (Session 5).

  Once a particular type of file is created it is displayed in the appropriate panel. Up to 200 filenames can be displayed in a panel.

- *File information.* The two lines near the bottom of the screen display information relating to the currently highlighted file. (At this point, no file is highlighted.)

- *Navigation line.* The navigation line at the bottom of the screen contains instructions for using the function keys to perform important commands, such as accessing help (F1), displaying the data stored in a file (F2), or activating the options in the menu bar (F10). The function keys are used throughout the dBASE menus to issue commands quickly.

THE DOT PROMPT

Once dBASE has been loaded into RAM, you can issue commands from either the Control Center (described in the last section) or from the dot prompt. When dBASE II and dBASE III (previous versions of dBASE) were loaded into RAM, all that appeared on the screen was a dot, referred to as the **dot prompt**. All commands had to be typed in after this prompt. To make dBASE easier to use, dBASE III Plus and dBASE IV incorporate a menu system that makes it unnecessary for the user to type in lengthy commands after the dot prompt. (dBASE IV's menu system is the Control Center.) Although all dBASE commands can be executed from the dot prompt, not all dBASE commands can be executed from the Control Center. Therefore, it is sometimes necessary to exit the Control Center to the dot prompt to issue a particular command. In the Changing the Current Drive section we lead you through exiting the Control Center menu to the dot prompt, issuing the drive change command from the dot prompt, and then displaying the Control Center.

USING THE MENUS

So that you can become familiar with dBASE's menu system, we lead you through using it to perform some fundamental procedures. In the sections below you learn how to use dBASE's menu system with both a keyboard and a mouse.

USING A KEYBOARD

As described in the last section, a menu bar displays at the top of Control Center screen. In addition, a menu bar displays at the top of most other DBASE screens. To move the highlight up to the menu bar so that you can access the menu options, either press F10 (as indicated on the bottom of the screen) or hold Alt down and type the letter of the menu option you want to access. Table 1.1 lists different methods for using dBASE's menu system.

Table 1.1 Methods for Using the Control Center With a Key- board	[F10]	Move the highlight to the menu; display the menu that was last used.
	[Alt] and the first letter of a menu name	Move the highlight to the pull-down menu that begins with the typed letter.
	[←], [→]	Display a pull-down menu to the left/right
	[↑], [↓], and then [Enter]	Highlight and then choose an option displaying in a pull-down menu
	[Esc]	Back out of a menu or a list of choices
	[Ctrl]+[End]	Save your work; accept certain menu assumptions
	[Tab]	Move the cursor to the right when columns are displaying
	[Shift]+[Tab]	Move the cursor to the left when columns are displaying
	[End]	Move the cursor to the bottom of a list
	[Home]	Move the cursor to the top of a list
	[PgDn]	Display next group of choices
	[PgUp]	Display previous group of choices

To practice the use of some of these keys, perform the following steps:

1. To move the highlight to the menu bar:
    PRESS: [F10]
    The screen should look like Figure 1.7, with the Catalog menu displaying.

2. To highlight the Tools menu:
    PRESS: [→]

3. To highlight the Exit menu:
    PRESS: [→]

Figure 1.7

Displaying the
Catalog menu.
Press F10 to
display the
menu bar.

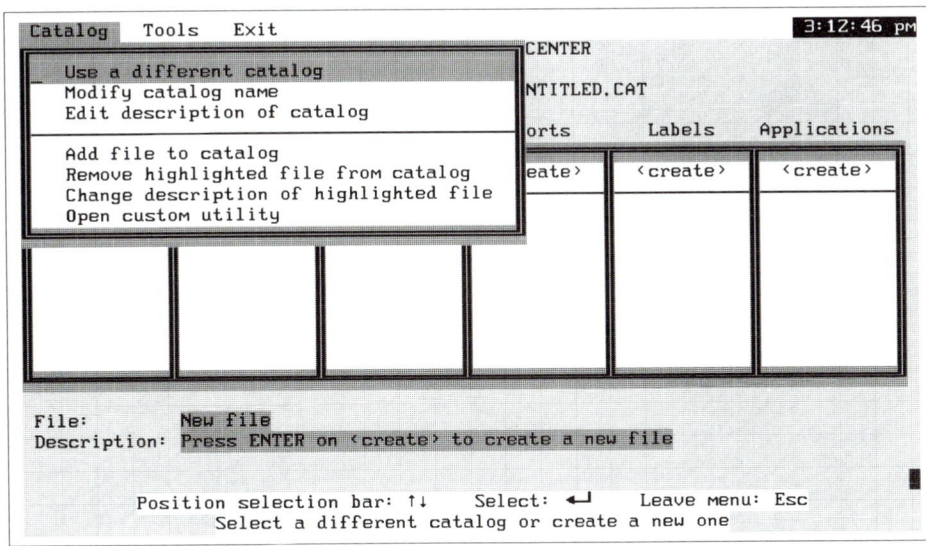

4. If you decide you don't want to display the menu bar:
   PRESS: Esc

5. To again display the menu bar:
   PRESS: F10
   Note that the Exit menu is now highlighted, whereas the Catalog menu
   was highlighted when you first activated the menu bar. *No matter what
   dBASE menu you use, dBASE will always display the last highlighted
   menu option.*

6. To remove the menu bar from the display:
   PRESS: Esc

7. To move directly to an option that is displaying in a menu bar, you can
   hold Alt down and type the first letter of the option. *Note*: The letter
   can be either uppercase or lowercase. For example, to highlight the
   Tools menu:
   PRESS: Alt+T
   The Tools menu should be displaying on the screen. *To choose a menu
   option in a pull-down menu, you can highlight it using the cursor-
   movement keys and then press* Enter.

8. So that the menu bar isn't displaying:
   PRESS: Esc

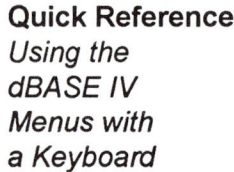

Quick Reference
*Using the
dBASE IV
Menus with
a Keyboard*

1. To display a pull-down menu, press `F10`, and then use `←` and `→` to highlight an adjacent pull-down menu; or hold `Alt` down and type the first letter of the pull-down menu you want to display.
2. Use `↑` and `↓` to highlight options within a pull-down menu. Press `Enter` to choose an option.
3. To back out of a menu:
   PRESS: `Esc`

USING A MOUSE

If you have a mouse connected to your computer and a mouse driver loaded in memory, dBASE will display a small rectangle, called the **mouse pointer**, on the screen. The mouse pointer moves around the screen when you roll the mouse on the surface of your desktop. Using dBASE IV, the mouse can be used to point to any menu option, a filename, or any item displaying in a list. To choose the highlighted item, click the left mouse button.

Note: In this guide we only provide instructions for using a keyboard. If you have a mouse connected to your computer, you may want to use the mouse to perform some of the procedures described.

USING HELP

If you need additional information about how to use a particular command, you can use dBASE's Help system. dBASE provides several methods for accessing Help information:

- Pressing `F1` from the Control Center.
- Typing HELP and then pressing `Enter` after the dot prompt.
- Choosing the Help button when an error box displays on the screen.

In the following steps you will practice using dBASE's Help system. You will access it by pressing `F1` from the Control Center. Perform the following steps:

1. The cursor should be highlighting the <create> marker in the Data panel.
   PRESS: F1
   The screen should look like Figure 1.8. Information relating to the current option is displaying in the Help box. At the bottom of the Help box, the following options are displaying:

Figure 1.8

The Help system

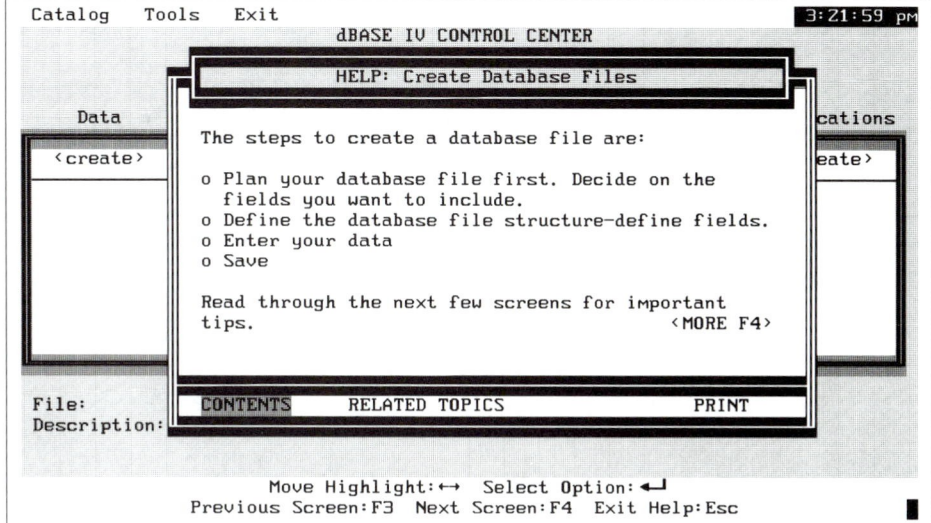

- CONTENTS. Choosing this option displays a Table of Contents that relates to the current panel.
- RELATED TOPICS. Choosing this option displays a list of topics that relate to the current one.
- PRINT. Choosing this option allows you to print the current Help screen out on the printer.

2. To display the Table of Contents that relates to the current panel, choose the CONTENTS option by highlighting it and then pressing Enter (this option may already be highlighted). The screen should look like Figure 1.9. When a new topic is chosen, the Help box displays text relating to the new topic. Table 1.2 lists different cursor-movement methods for using the CONTENTS box.

Figure 1.9

Using the
Help system's
Table of cont-
ents option

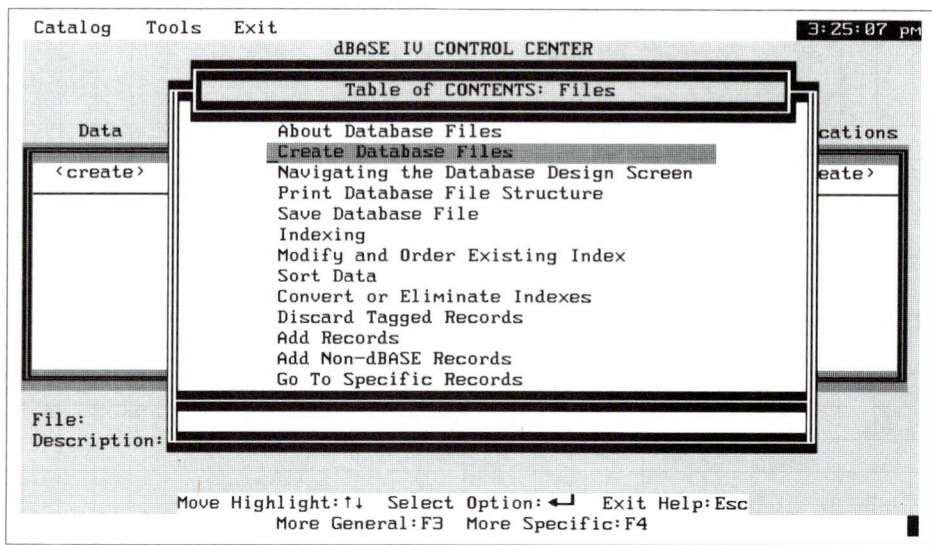

3. So that this screen no longer displays:
    PRESS: [Esc]
    The Control Center should again be displaying.

4. To initiate the HELP command again so that you can use the
    RELATED TOPICS option:
    PRESS: [F1]

Table 1.2

Moving the Cursor
in the CONTENTS
Help Box

[F3] Previous	Display a broader level of topic detail
[F4] Next	Display a more detailed description of topics or move the cursor up and down in a list of topics
[PgUp] and [PgDn]	Display a list of topics, a box at at time
[Home]	Move to the top of a list
[End]	Move to the bottom of a list

---

5. Choose the RELATED TOPICS option by highlighting it and then
    pressing [Enter]. A list of topics should be displaying that relate to the
    current topic. (At this point, the current topic relates to creating
    database files.)

6. To exit Help:
   PRESS: [Esc] *twice*

Quick Reference
Using Help

Pressing [F1] will display information relating to the currently highlighted dBASE IV menu option. To exit the Help system, press [Esc] to display the last dBASE screen you were working on.

CHANGING THE CURRENT DRIVE

Before you create the structure for a database in the next section, we will lead you through changing the current drive so dBASE knows you will be saving your work onto the Advantage Diskette. The current assumption made by dBASE is to save and retrieve using the hard disk. *Note*: Since some computer systems are configured with both a 3.5-inch and a 5.25-inch disk drive or drives of different storage capacities, you will need to insert the Advantage Diskette in either drive A: or drive B:, depending on the size and storage capacity of your Advantage Diskette.

Perform the following steps:

1. The Control Center should be displaying on the screen.

2. Insert the Advantage Diskette in the appropriate diskette drive. (*Note*: If you're not sure whether to use drive A: or drive B:, ask your instructor or lab assistant.)

3. To display the dot prompt:
   TYPE: [Alt]+E
   To choose the Exit to dot prompt option:
   PRESS: [Enter]
   The dot prompt should be displaying.

4. If your Advantage Diskette is in drive A:, type SET DIRECTORY TO A: and then press [Enter]. If your Advantage Diskette is in drive B:, type SET DIRECTORY TO B: and then press [Enter].

5. The dot prompt should again be displaying on the screen. To display the Control Center:

TYPE: ASSIST
PRESS: Enter
dBASE now knows it will save and retrieve using the Advantage Diskette that is located in either drive A: or drive B:.

THE DATABASE STRUCTURE

In this section we lead you through creating the structure for the CUSTOMER database—that is, defining the characteristics of each field to be included in the database. In addition, we lead you through modifying and printing the database structure.

CREATING THE DATABASE STRUCTURE

The structure of the CUSTOMER database is pictured in Figure 1.10. We described what to consider when creating a database in the DBMS Features section earlier in this session. Perform the following steps:

Figure 1.10

The structure of the CUSTOMER database

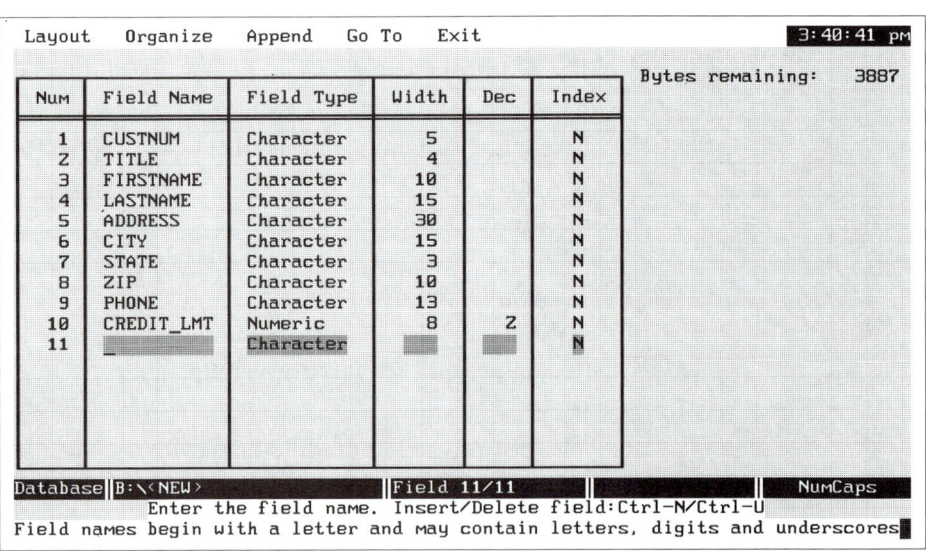

```
   Layout    Organize    Append    Go To    Exit                    3:40:41 PM
                                                    Bytes remaining:    3887
  ┌─────┬──────────────┬────────────┬───────┬─────┬───────┐
  │ Num │  Field Name  │ Field Type │ Width │ Dec │ Index │
  ├─────┼──────────────┼────────────┼───────┼─────┼───────┤
  │  1  │ CUSTNUM      │ Character  │   5   │     │   N   │
  │  2  │ TITLE        │ Character  │   4   │     │   N   │
  │  3  │ FIRSTNAME    │ Character  │  10   │     │   N   │
  │  4  │ LASTNAME     │ Character  │  15   │     │   N   │
  │  5  │ ADDRESS      │ Character  │  30   │     │   N   │
  │  6  │ CITY         │ Character  │  15   │     │   N   │
  │  7  │ STATE        │ Character  │   3   │     │   N   │
  │  8  │ ZIP          │ Character  │  10   │     │   N   │
  │  9  │ PHONE        │ Character  │  13   │     │   N   │
  │ 10  │ CREDIT_LMT   │ Numeric    │   8   │  2  │   N   │
  │ 11  │              │ Character  │       │     │   N   │
  └─────┴──────────────┴────────────┴───────┴─────┴───────┘

 Database│B:\<NEW>                       │Field 11/11              │  NumCaps
              Enter the field name. Insert/Delete field:Ctrl-N/Ctrl-U
 Field names begin with a letter and may contain letters, digits and underscores
```

1. The Control Center should be displaying on the screen. Highlight the <create> marker in the Data panel. Press Enter.

2. The screen should now look like Figure 1.11. When you type in the specifications for the structure of the database, dBASE will convert all your letters to uppercase.

Figure 1.11

To create a database structure, you must type the specifications into this screen.

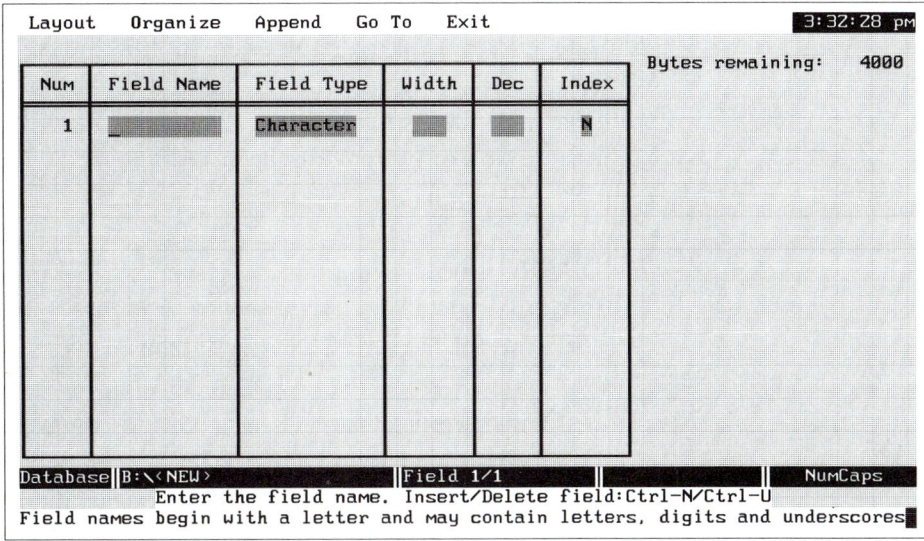

TYPE: CUSTNUM
PRESS: Enter
The cursor is now positioned in the Type column. Note that dBASE indicates (below the status line on the bottom of the screen) that you can change the field type by pressing the Space Bar. (Field types were described earlier in the DBMS Features section.) Even though you want this field to be defined as Character, practice changing the information that displays in the Field Type column.
PRESS: Space Bar *to change the type to Numeric*
PRESS: Space Bar *to change the type to Float*
PRESS: Space Bar *until the field type displays "Character" again*
Note: You can also change the field type by typing the first character of the type you want. For example, if you want a field to be numeric, you could type N while the cursor is positioned in the Type column.

3. The cursor should be positioned in the Type column and the text "Character" should be displaying. To move the cursor to the Width column:
PRESS: Enter

4. To specify a width of 5:
    TYPE: 5
    PRESS: [Enter]
    Note that dBASE didn't prompt you to enter anything in the Dec
    column. dBASE will only prompt you for the number of decimals when
    defining the characteristics of Numeric and Float field types.

5. The cursor is now positioned in the Index column. Indexing on a
    certain field enables you to put the database into order by that field
    (that is, once data has been added). For now, you will accept dBASE's
    assumption of N. Indexing is described in Session 2.
    PRESS: [Enter]

6. DBASE is now prompting you to enter field information for the second
    field in the database. By referring to Figure 1.10, type in the rest of the
    structure for the CUSTOMER database.

    Note that the ZIP and CUSTNUM fields were defined as Character
    field types rather than Numeric field types. This is because calculations
    won't be performed on those fields. For example, you wouldn't want to
    calculate the average ZIP code or the total of all customer numbers.

To save the CUSTOMER database structure, perform the following steps:

1. To display the Exit menu:
    PRESS: [Alt]+E
    The cursor is currently highlighting the Save changes and exit option.
    To choose this option:
    PRESS: [Enter]

2. dBASE is now prompting you to type in a name for the database. It
    doesn't matter if you use upper- or lowercase letters.
    a. The Advantage Diskette should be in the appropriate diskette drive
        (if necessary, see Changing the Current Drive section).
    b. TYPE: CUSTOMER
        PRESS: [Enter]

    The CUSTOMER database structure has now been saved onto the
    Advantage Diskette. *Note*: You didn't need to type A: or B: before the
    filename because you changed the current drive to drive A: or drive B:
    in the last section.

    The Control Center should be displaying on the screen. The cursor is
    highlighting the CUSTOMER filename in the Data panel. *Note*: The

horizontal line is now below the CUSTOMER filename. This indicates that the database is now in use. If other databases were stored on your disk, they would be listed below this horizontal line.

Quick Reference *Creating a* *Database* *Structure*	1. With the Control Center displaying, highlight the <create> marker in the Data panel, and then press (Enter). 2. Type in the specifications for the database structure. 3. To save your specifications, activate the Exit menu, and then choose the Save changes and exit option.

MODIFYING THE DATABASE STRUCTURE

dBASE IV allows you to change the structure of an existing database file by either adding or deleting fields or changing the characteristics of a field (such as field width). When you invoke this command, dBASE makes a temporary backup copy of the database file to be modified. After you've made changes to the structure, dBASE asks you to confirm your changes.

In this section, you will change the width of the FIRSTNAME field from 10 to 12 (to accommodate longer first names). Perform the following steps:

1. Highlight CUSTOMER in the Data panel, and then press (Enter).

2. Choose the Modify structure/order option. The options in the menu that is currently displaying are used when you want to make changes that affect the indexing of the database.

3. Since you don't need to use any of the options in this menu:
   PRESS: (Esc)

4. Using the cursor-movement keys, position the cursor in the width column of the FIRSTNAME field.

5. With the cursor in the width column of the FIRSTNAME field:
   TYPE: 12
   PRESS: (Enter)

6. To activate the Exit menu so you can save the change you made to the structure of the CUSTOMER database:
   PRESS: (Alt)+E

7. Choose the Save changes and exit option.

8. dBASE now asks if you're sure you want to make changes. To choose
    the Yes option:
    PRESS: (Enter)
    The Control Center should be displaying on the screen.

Quick Reference   1. From the Control Center, highlight the name of the database you
Modifying the   want to modify in the Data panel, and then press (Enter).
Database   2. Choose the Modify structure/order option.
Structure   3. Make your changes.
                        4. To save your changes, activate the Exit menu and then choose the
                            Save changes and exit option. Then choose the Yes option.

PRINTING THE DATABASE STRUCTURE

Once you have modified or created a database structure, you may want to
print it so you can review its characteristics.

To display the CUSTOMER database structure, perform the following
tasks:

1. Make sure your computer is attached to a printer and that the printer
    has been turned on.

2. Highlight CUSTOMER in the Data panel, and then press (Enter).

3. Choose the Modify structure/order option.

4. The Organize menu should be displaying on the screen. Highlight the
    Layout menu by pressing (←).

5. The cursor should be highlighting the Print database structure option.
    PRESS: (Enter)

6. To begin printing:
    PRESS: (Enter)
    The database structure should be printing on the printer. Note that the
    FIRSTNAME field now has a width of 12.

7. To exit back to the Control Center, choose either option in the Exit menu (depending on whether you made changes to the database).

....

Quick Reference   1. Choose the appropriate file name in the Data panel.
Printing the   2. Choose the Modify structure/order option.
Database   3. Display the Layout menu.
Structure   4. Choose the Print database structure option.
                       5. Choose the Begin printing option.

....

EXITING dBASE IV

One of the most important DBMS functions to learn is how to exit. With dBASE IV, when you exit the program properly, all your database management activities (such as adding or deleting activities) are automatically saved in the database. *If you turn off your computer without exiting dBASE, you may lose data.* Always exit dBASE at the end of each working session.

Perform the following procedure:

1. To exit dBASE, activate the Exit menu from the Control Center:
    TYPE: [Alt]+E

2. Choose the Quit to DOS option.
    You should see the DOS prompt on the screen.

3. To load dBASE IV again:
    TYPE: dbase
    PRESS: [Enter]
    The Control Center should again be displaying on the screen. Note that the name CUSTOMER now appears below the line in the Data panel. This is because when you first load the program, dBASE doesn't know what database you're working with. In the next section, we lead you through telling dBASE what database file you want to work with.

Quick Reference
Exiting
dBASE IV   Choose the Quit to DOS option from the Exit menu of the Control
                                Center.

Because you exited dBASE, you need to again specify that you want to
save your work onto the Advantage Diskette that is located in either drive
A: or drive B:. Otherwise it will think you want to save your work onto the
hard disk. To do this, perform the following steps (these steps were
described earlier):

1. The Control Center should be displaying on the screen.

2. Insert the Advantage Diskette in the appropriate diskette drive. (*Note*:
    If you're not sure whether to use drive A: or drive B:, ask your
    instructor or lab assistant.)

3. To display the dot prompt:
    TYPE: Alt+E
    To choose the Exit to dot prompt option:
    PRESS: Enter
    The dot prompt should be displaying.

4. If your Advantage Diskette is in drive A:, type SET DIRECTORY TO
    A: and then press Enter. If your Advantage Diskette is in drive B:,
    type SET DIRECTORY TO B: and then press Enter.

5. The dot prompt should again be displaying on the screen. To display
    the Control Center:
    TYPE: ASSIST
    PRESS: Enter
    dBASE now knows it will save and retrieve using the Advantage
    Diskette that is located in either drive A: or drive B:.

USING A DATABASE AND ADDING RECORDS

You should now be viewing the Control Center. If you completed the last
section (Exiting dBASE IV), dBASE doesn't know what database you
want to work with. Although you probably have only one database stored

on the Advantage Diskette, most business tasks involve the use of many databases. Therefore, dBASE requires that you specify what database you want to work with at the beginning of each working session. This is similar in concept to deciding what drawer in a filing cabinet you want to open.

Perform the following steps to use the CUSTOMER database:

1. Highlight CUSTOMER in the Data panel, and then press (Enter).

2. Choose the Use file option. The name CUSTOMER now appears above the line in the Data panel. In addition, the name CUSTOMER appears on the bottom of the screen. Any commands you issue right now will pertain to the CUSTOMER database until you either create or use another database file.

Quick Reference
Using a
Database

1. Highlight the name of the database in the Data panel and then press (Enter).
2. Choose the Use file option.

At this point, you know you are using the CUSTOMER database because the name CUSTOMER is displaying above the line in the Data panel. In this section you will add the records pictured in Figure 1.12 to the CUSTOMER database.

Note: Adding records to a database you have just created is accomplished by pressing (F2) (Data). After records have been added to a database, this key is also used to edit, or make changes to, database records. After the first group of records have been added to a database, you must activate the Records menu after pressing (F2) in order to add records in subsequent sessions.

Perform the following steps:

1. To add records:
   PRESS: (F2)
   The screen should look like Figure 1.13.

2. The cursor should be blinking in the CUSTNUM field. A note about entering data: If you fill up a field with data, dBASE will beep and automatically move the cursor to the next field. If you don't fill up a

field with data, press (Enter) to move the cursor to the next field. Key in the following data:

```
5410               (Enter)
Mr.                (Enter)
Sean               (Enter)
Dennis             (Enter)
132 Walnut Lane    (Enter)
San Francisco      (Enter)
CA                 (Enter)
94122              (Enter)
415-441-3222       (Enter)
2500               (Enter)
```

Figure 1.12

CUSTOMER database listing

Record#	CUSTNUM	TITLE	FIRSTNAME	LASTNAME
1	5410	Mr.	Sean	Dennis
2	4809	Ms.	Veronica	Visentin
3	4999	Mr.	Charles	Cattermole
4	3906	Mr.	Frank	Chihowski
5	6211	Ms.	Heidi	Buehre
6	4500	Ms.	Joellen	Baldwin
7	5100	Ms.	Lynne	Morrow-Tabacchi
8	5807	Mr.	Samuel	Hussey
9	3909	Ms.	Rosalie	Skears
10	5140	Ms.	Joan	Vieau

Record#	ADDRESS	CITY	STATE	ZIP
1	132 Walnut Lane	San Francisco	CA	94122
2	90 Spruce Street	San Mateo	CA	94019
3	18 Cameo Road	San Francisco	CA	94102
4	9 Bye Street	San Francisco	CA	94102
5	3255 S. Parker Road #1-605	San Mateo	CA	94019
6	2729 Glen Ellen Drive	San Francisco	CA	94102
7	11322 Overlook Drive N E	San Mateo	CA	94019
8	23 Linlew Drive, Apt. 15	San Mateo	CA	94102
9	9504 Wellington Street	San Mateo	CA	94102
10	55 Francisco Street	San Francisco	CA	94109

Record#	PHONE	CREDIT_LMT
1	415-441-3222	2500.00
2	415-342-3988	2000.00
3	415-474-0987	250.00
4	415-981-7881	3500.00
5	415-344-2355	2500.00
6	415-343-2105	1500.00
7	415-342-4655	3000.00
8	415-344-5661	2500.00
9	415-342-3766	3000.00
10	415-474-4554	1500.00

Figure 1.13

Adding data to
the CUSTOMER
database.

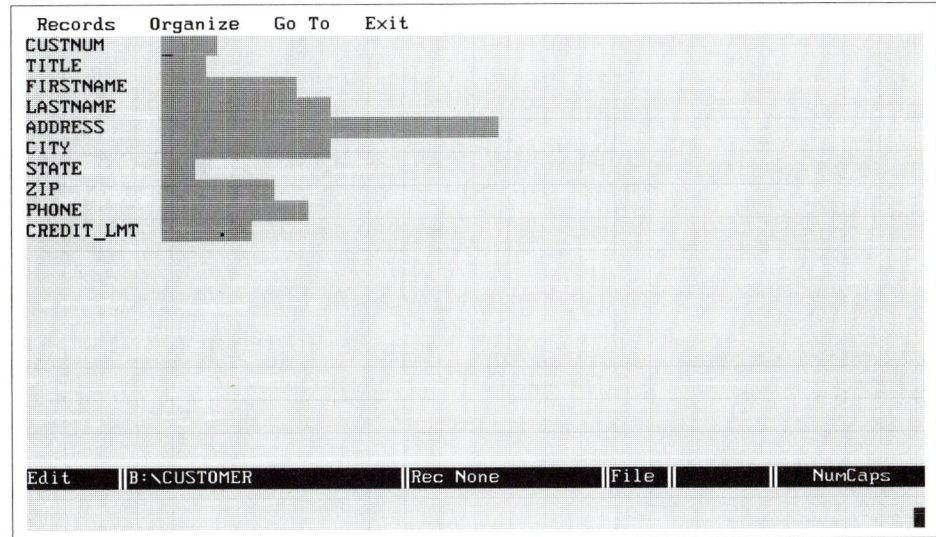

3. (If dBASE asks if you want to add new records, type Y.) dBASE should now be waiting for you to enter information into the second record. What if you made a mistake when entering data into the first record? Fortunately, dBASE provides a number of methods for moving to records and within records. For practice, perform the following step.

4. To move the cursor to the beginning of the first record:
PRESS: [PgUp]
The cursor should now be positioned beneath the "5" of "5410."

5. Press [↓] four times to move the cursor to the ADDRESS field. If you wanted to make changes at this point you could simply retype the contents of this field. Whereas [↑] and [↓] are used to move from field to field, [←] and [→] are used to move from character to character within fields. If you want to delete a character, position the cursor on the character and press [Delete]. If you want to insert a character, or characters, press [Insert]. (Note that when you press [Insert], the status line indicates that Insert mode has been activated.)

6. To move the cursor to the next record to enter data:
PRESS: [PgDn]
If dBASE asks if you want to add new records:
TYPE: Y
Note: After you use what dBASE considers to be an editing command, if your cursor is on the last record of the database, dBASE will ask if you want to add records.

7. Refer to Figure 1.12 to enter the rest of the data into the CUSTOMER file. You may want to choose the Add new records option from the Records menu before proceeding. When you have entered the last record and your cursor is on a blank record, proceed with the next step.

8. Since you are finished entering all the data into this database, it is time to return to the Control Center. However, if you exit the CUSTOMER file while your cursor is positioned on a blank record, you will save a blank record along with your database. Before exiting, always press (PgUp) so your cursor is on a record that contains data. (*Note*: Here you are exiting a file to return to the Control Center; you are not exiting dBASE altogether.)
    PRESS: (PgUp)

CAUTION: Always press (PgUp) so your cursor is on a record that contains data before exiting to the Control Center. Otherwise a blank record will be saved along with your database.

9. To exit to the Control Center, you must first activate the menus:
    PRESS: (F10)

10. Highlight the Exit menu (by pressing (→)).

11. Choose the Exit option. The Control Center should be displaying on the screen.

DISPLAYING DATA AND EDITING

dBASE provides several methods for displaying and editing the data stored in your database. The simplest method involves pressing (F2) (Data) while viewing the Control Center. (We describe other methods for displaying and editing in Session 3.) When first pressed, (F2) will display only the current record on the screen so that you can edit it (Figure 1.14). This display mode is referred to as **Edit mode**. Depending on which record is current, display additional records by pressing (PgUp) or (PgDn). If the cursor is on the last record of the database, pressing (PgDn) will cause dBASE to ask if you want to add additional records. You can respond by typing either Y or N.

Quick Reference
Adding
Records
1. After activating, or using, a database:
   PRESS: (F2)
2. Activate the Records menu.
3. Choose the Add new records option.
4. Save the newly added records by first positioning the cursor on a record that contains data and then activating the Exit menu. Choose the Exit option.

Figure 1.14

Edit mode

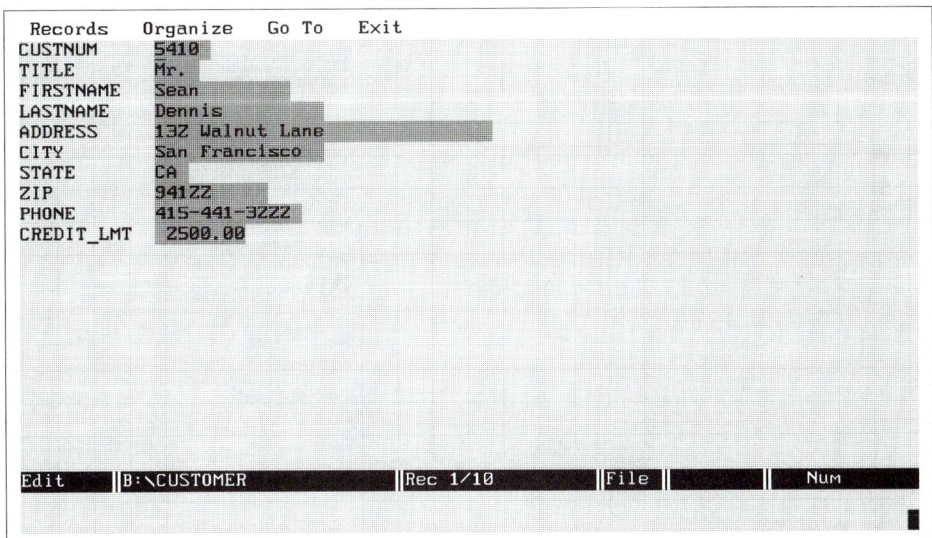

Many people prefer to use **Browse mode** when displaying or editing data. In this mode, records are displayed horizontally in the form of a table so that you can see more than one record at a time (Figure 1.15). To display your data in Browse mode, press (F2) while viewing your data in Edit mode. *(F2) is a toggle key that displays your data in either Edit or Browse mode, depending on which mode you used last.* In Browse mode you can use (Tab) to move the cursor across the screen to the right and (Shift)+(Tab) to move the cursor across the screen to the left. (↑) and (↓) will move the cursor up and down through the database records. As in Edit mode, if you press (↓) while the cursor is on the last record of the database, dBASE will ask if you want to add data.

You can edit your data while in Edit mode or Browse mode by moving the cursor to the record and field you want to edit and then typing in your changes. *If you do make changes while in Edit or Browse mode, you will need to save your changes by activating the Exit menu and then choosing the Exit option. If you don't make changes, you can simply press* **Esc** *to exit to the Control Center.*

Perform the following steps to practice using **F2**:

1. To display the data stored in the CUSTOMER database in either Edit or Browse mode:
   PRESS: **F2**

Figure 1.15

Browse mode

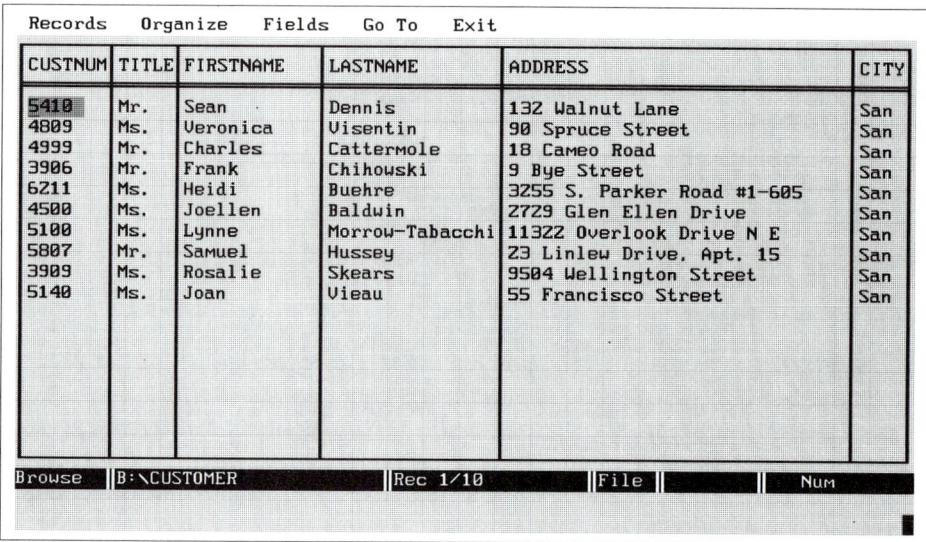

2. To change the mode of display:
   PRESS: **F2**

3. Press **F2** until you are viewing the data in Browse mode. Then practice using **Tab** and **Shift**+**Tab** to move from field to field in the Browse screen.

4. To exit the Control Center without saving (since you haven't made any changes):
   PRESS: **Esc**

Quick Reference
Displaying
Data and
Editing

1. Highlight the name of a database file in the Data panel of the Control Center.
2. Press F2 to display the data in either Edit or Browse mode. To display the data in a different mode, press F2 again.
3. In Browse mode, to move the cursor to a field located to the right, press Tab. To move the cursor to a field located to the left, press Shift+Tab.
4. If you make changes to the database in either Edit or Browse mode, activate the Exit menu and choose the Exit option. Otherwise press Esc to display the Control Center.

PRINTING A DATABASE LISTING

To print a list of the records stored in your database, use the QUICK REPORT command (Shift+F9) while highlighting a database name in the Data panel of the Control Center or while displaying the database in either Edit or Browse mode. (In Sessions 3–4, we describe additional methods for printing your database.) *Note*: dBASE prints your database beginning with the first field. If the database is to wide to fit across the width of the paper, some fields will be omitted from the listing. (In Session 3, we describe how to list selective fields on the screen.)

If you are viewing the Control Center, the steps for printing a database listing include:

1. Highlight a database name in the Data panel of the Control Center.

2. To initiate the QUICK REPORT command:
    PRESS: Shift+F9

3. To begin printing, choose the Begin printing option. Press Esc to cancel printing.

If you are viewing a database in either Edit or Browse mode, the steps for printing the database listing include:

1. To initiate the QUICK REPORT command:
    PRESS: Shift+F9

2. To begin printing, choose the Begin printing option. Press (Esc) to cancel printing.

Note: If you choose the View report on screen option instead of the Begin printing option, your database will list on the screen. When a database is too wide to fit on the screen, the screen display becomes confused because the field data wraps around to the next line. (As mentioned previously, Session 3 describes how you can be selective about the fields that list.)

....

Quick Reference   If you are viewing the Control Center:
Printing a Database   1. Highlight a database name in the Data panel.
Listing   2. PRESS: (Shift)+(F9)
                             3. Choose the Begin printing option.

                             If you are displaying a database in either Edit or Browse mode:
                             1. PRESS: (Shift)+(F9)
                             2. Choose the Begin printing option.

....

ORGANIZING DATABASE FILES WITH CATALOGS

As you work with dBASE over time, the number of files you create and use will likely increase. As mentioned earlier in this session, a **catalog** provides a means by which you can group, and display in the Control Center, database files that belong together. For example, a sporting goods company might want to use one catalog to group inventory-related database files, and another to group employee-related database files. Without the use of an inventory catalog, all the inventory-related files will be listed along with the employee-related files. If you use an inventory catalog, only those files that relate to inventory will list in the Control Center. If you are using dBASE to manage only one group of related files, you won't find it necessary to organize your database files with catalogs.

THE INITIAL CATALOG

When you load dBASE, the catalog you were last using becomes the active catalog. If you haven't created any catalogs, dBASE creates one for you and names it "untitled." If you want, you can rename it by choosing the Modify catalog name option from the Catalog menu.

CREATING A CATALOG AND ADDING FILES

To create a catalog, you must choose the Use a different catalog option from the Catalog menu. Then highlight the <create> marker and press [Enter]. dBASE will then prompt you to type a name for the catalog. A catalog name can be between one and eight characters; letters, numbers, and underscores can be used in catalog names, but punctuation marks and blanks cannot. After typing in the catalog name, press [Enter]. The Control Center will again display, but all the panels will be empty.

Quick Reference
Creating a
Catalog

1. Choose the Use a different catalog option from the Catalog menu.
2. Highlight the <create> marker and press [Enter].
3. Type a name for the catalog and then press [Enter].

To add a file to a catalog, first position the cursor in the panel to which you want to add a file. Choose the Add file to catalog option from the Catalog menu. Only those files that can go into the current panel will display. For example, if the cursor is in the Reports panel, a list of report files will display on the screen. Highlight the file you want to add and then press [Enter]. Continue in this fashion until all the related files have been added to the current catalog.

Quick Reference
Adding Files
to a Catalog

1. Position the cursor in the panel to which you want to add a file.
2. Choose the Add file to catalog option from the Catalog menu. A list of the files that can go into the current panel will display.
3. Highlight the file you want to add and press [Enter].

USING A DIFFERENT CATALOG

To use a different catalog, you must choose the Use a different catalog option from the Catalog menu. Highlight the catalog you want to use and press [Enter].

Quick Reference
Using a Different Catalog

1. Choose the Use a different catalog option from the Catalog menu.
2. Highlight the catalog you want to use and press `Enter`.

REMOVING FILES FROM A CATALOG

To remove a file from a catalog, first highlight the file you want to remove. Then choose the Remove highlighted file from catalog option from the Catalog menu. Then press `Delete`. dBASE will then prompt you to make sure you want to actually remove the file from the catalog. If you do, choose the Yes option. dBASE will then ask if you want to remove the file from the disk. Choose the No option.

Quick Reference
Removing Files from a Catalog

1. Highlight the file you want to remove.
2. Choose the Remove highlighted file from catalog option from the Catalog menu.
3. PRESS: `Delete`
4. To remove the file from the catalog, choose the Yes option.
5. dBASE will now ask if you want to remove the file from the disk. Choose the No option.

SUMMARY

In this session you learned how to create the structure for a database and add data to the database. When creating a structure you must define the characteristics of each field in the database. Specifically, you must define the field name, field type, width, and number of decimal places (for numeric fields) for each field in the database. Although you can later modify the structure of a database, it is a good idea to give careful thought to the setup of the structure before you create it and then add records.

Saving a database is accomplished by exiting dBASE—always exit dBASE properly to save the database you're using. Then, after reloading dBASE at a later point, you must highlight the name of a database in the Data panel and press `Enter` to tell dBASE what database you want to work with.

COMMAND SUMMARY

The table on the next few pages provides a list of the commands and procedures covered in this session.

Table 1.3 Command Summary	Creating a Database Structure	1. With the Control Center displaying, highlight the <create> marker in the Data panel, and then press Enter. 2. Type in the specifications for the database structure. 3. To save your specifications, activate the Exit menu, and then choose the Save changes and exit option.
	Modifying the Database Structure	1. From the Control Center, highlight the name of the database you want to modify in the Data panel, and then press Enter. 2. Choose the Modify structure/order option. 3. Make your changes. 4. To save your changes, activate the Exit menu and then choose the Save changes and exit option. Then choose the Yes option.
	Printing the Database Structure	1. Choose the appropriate file name in the Data panel. 2. Choose the Modify structure/order option. 3. Display the Layout menu. 4. Choose the Print database structure option. 5. Choose the Begin printing option.
	Exiting dBASE IV	Choose the Quit to DOS option from the Exit menu of the Control Center.
	Using a Database	Highlight the name of the database in the Data panel and then press Enter. Choose the Use file option.

Table 1.3 Command Summary (continued)	Using Help	Press F1 to display information relating to the currently highlighted dBASE IV menu option. To exit the help system, press Esc to display the last dBASE screen you were working on.
	Adding Records	1. After activating, or using, a database: PRESS: F2 2. Activate the Records menu. 3. Choose the Add new records option. 4. Save the newly added records by first positioning the cursor on a record that contains data and then activating the Exit menu. Choose the Exit option.
	Displaying Data and Editing	1. Highlight the name of a database file in the Data panel of the Control Center. 2. Press F2 to display the data in either Edit or Browse mode. To display the data in a different mode, press F2 again. 3. In Browse mode, to move the cursor to a field located to the right, press Tab. To move the cursor to a field located to the left, press Shift+Tab. 4. If you make changes to the database in either Edit or Browse mode, activate the Exit menu and choose the Exit option. Otherwise press Esc to display the Control Center.

Table 1.3	Printing a Database Listing	If you are viewing the Control Center:
Command Summary (concluded)		1. Highlight a database name in the Data panel. 2. PRESS: [Shift]+[F9] 3. Choose the Begin printing option. If you are displaying a database in either Edit or Browse mode: 1. PRESS: [Shift]+[F9] 2. Choose the Begin printing option.

KEY TERMS

arithmetic operations   The operations of addition, subtraction, multiplication, division, and exponentiation.

Browse mode   In dBASE IV, this mode enables you to see database records in rows on the screen; this mode is used for editing records in a database. *See* Edit mode.

catalog   In dBASE IV, catalogs provide a means by which the user can group related database files.

character   In dBASE IV, data that is nonnumeric.

Control Center   The center of dBASE IV's menu system.

<create> marker   In dBASE IV, a feature of each panel; used to create a file (a different dBASE screen displays for each panel chosen).

database   Large group of stored, integrated (cross-referenced) data that can be retrieved and manipulated to produce information.

database management system (DBMS)   Comprehensive software tool that allows users to create, maintain, and manipulate an integrated base of business data to produce relevant management information. A DBMS represents the interface between the user and the computer's operating system and database.

database structure   The characteristics of every field stored in a database.

date   In dBASE IV, data that must be entered in a specific date format so that calculations can be performed on it.

dot prompt   In dBASE IV, when the user exits the Control Center, a dot displays on the screen. Commands can be typed after this prompt.

Edit mode   In dBASE IV, this mode enables the user to see one database record one at a time on the screen; this mode is used for editing the records in a database. *See* Browse mode.

field name   In a database structure, the unique name given to each field of data that is stored. A field name can be no longer than 10 characters.

field type   In a database structure, the specification of the kind of data that will be stored in a given field (character, numeric, date, logical, float, or memo).

field width   In a database structure, the width of each field must be defined by the user.

float   Field type in dBASE IV. Floating point numbers are typically used in scientific applications.

index file   In dBASE IV, this file contains a series of pointers that enable the user to display a database file in a different order.

logical   Field type in dBASE IV. Logical fields contain true or false data.

logical operations   Operations consisting oof three common comparisons: equal to, less than, and greater than. Two common words used in basic logical operations are AND and OR.

memo   Field type in dBASE IV. Memo fields contain data in a long paragraph of text.

mouse pointer   If you use a mouse with your computer, dBASE displays a small rectangle as a mouse pointer that you can move around the screen to highlight items for selection.

nonnumeric   Character data, or data that doesn't contain numbers. Calculations can't be performed on nonnumeric data.

numeric   Field type in dBASE IV. Numeric data can be used in calculations, such as dollar amounts.

panels   Six vertical sections in dBASE IV's Control Center that make up most of the screen; each panel enables the user to create a different type of file with specific capabilities.

relational operations   A relational operation compares two elements of data to determine if one element is greater than, less than, or equal to the other.

searches   With database software, you can perform searches of your database to retrieve specific information.

EXERCISES

SHORT ANSWER

1. What are the basic components of the dBASE IV Control Center?
2. When you are ready to stop working with dBASE, what must you always do to save your database file(s)?
3. What is a database management system?
4. When you first load dBASE, what must you do before you can begin working on a database?
5. When might you find it useful to create and add files to a catalog?
6. What is involved in modifying a database structure? Why might you want to do this?
7. Being able to create stylized reports of your data is an important capability. How does a report listing of your database differ from a "regular" listing of the fields in your database?
8. Describe the six types of data you can store in a database.
9. What is the dot prompt and why is it relevant to know how to display it?
10. What is the difference between Browse mode and Edit mode? How do you display data in one of these modes?

HANDS-ON

1. In this step you will create the EMPLOYEE database and add records to it, modify and print the database structure, and edit a few records. Perform the following steps:
   a. Create the structure for the EMPLOYEE database. The structure is pictured in Figure 1.1 (refer to the beginning of the session).
   b. Add the records pictured in Figure 1.2 to the EMPLOYEE database.
   c. Save the database permanently by exiting dBASE.
   d. Load dBASE. Use the EMPLOYEE database.
   e. Modify the structure for the EMPLOYEE database by changing the width of the STATE field to 3. (Because of this change, dBASE won't beep when you add STATE field data, since the field width (3) is now longer than the data that you will be putting into this field.)
   f. Display the structure of the EMPLOYEE database on the screen.
   g. Make up data for two more records and then add them to the EMPLOYEE database.
   h. You've decided to give all of your employees a raise of $1.00 per hour. Display the EMPLOYEE database in Browse mode and edit the database to include the new hourly wages.
   i. Rosalie Gills's address has changed. Her new address is:
      146 Sanchez, San Francisco, CA, 94115
   j. Print a listing of the EMPLOYEE database using the QUICK REPORTS command. (*Note*: Since the database is too wide to fit on the paper, only the first few fields will be included in the listing).

2. To practice creating a database structure, adding records, and then listing the database, perform the following steps:
   a. Create the INVENT database on the Advantage Diskette. The structure for the database is pictured in Figure 1.16.
   b. Add the records pictured in Figure 1.17 to the INVENT database.
   c. Display the INVENT database in Browse mode.
   d. Print a listing of the INVENT database.

Figure 1.16

The INVENT database structure

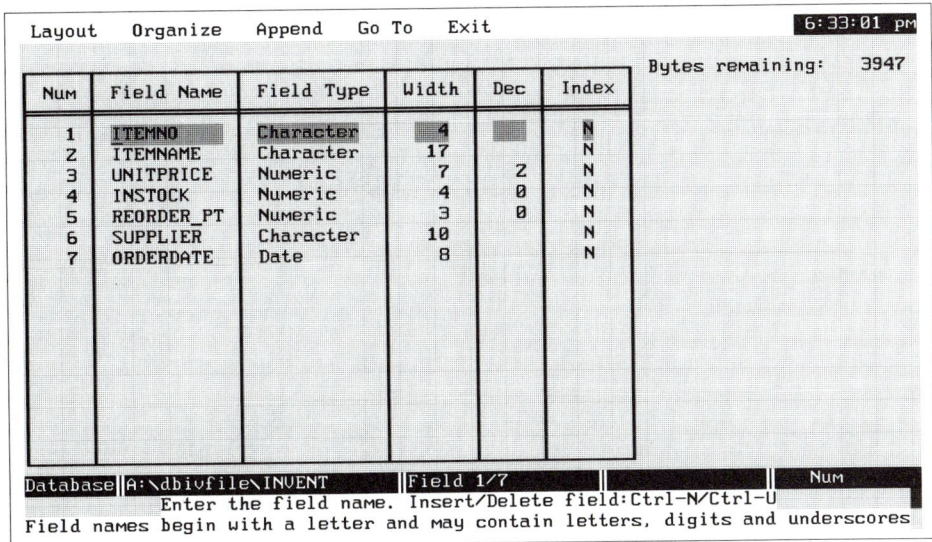

Figure 1.17

The INVENT database records

ITEMNO	ITEMNAME	UNITPRICE	INSTOCK	REORDER_PT	SUPPLIER	ORDERDATE
401	HAMMER	15.68	37	10	ADAMS	05/16/92
209	SHOVEL	19.99	4	5	ADAMS	04/17/92
215	NAILS	4.50	15	20	ZENA	04/25/92
289	BROOM	7.89	22	5	PARNELL	03/15/92
360	SCREW DRIVER	3.99	42	20	ADAMS	06/20/92
300	VACUUM CLEANER	89.99	3	5	PARNELL	05/02/92
299	BATTERIES	3.59	25	20	PARNELL	06/01/92
411	LIGHT BULBS	2.99	55	15	ZENA	07/03/92
399	WRENCH	11.99	12	10	ADAMS	05/15/92
355	MASKING TAPE	1.99	17	10	ZENA	06/01/92
288	HOE	19.99	19	10	ADAMS	05/05/92
366	WOOD STAIN	5.99	35	5	PARNELL	04/21/92
405	CARPET CLEANER	7.99	21	5	ZENA	06/15/92
309	DUST SPRAY	4.21	32	10	ZENA	05/29/92
280	BATHROOM CLEANER	2.99	41	15	PARNELL	06/15/92

Browse ‖A:\dbivfile\<NEW> ‖Rec 1/15 ‖View ‖ Num

3. To practice creating a database structure and then adding records, perform the following steps:

   a. Create the EXPENSES database on your data diskette. The structure for the database is pictured in Figure 1.18.

Figure 1.18

The EXPENSES
database struc-
ture

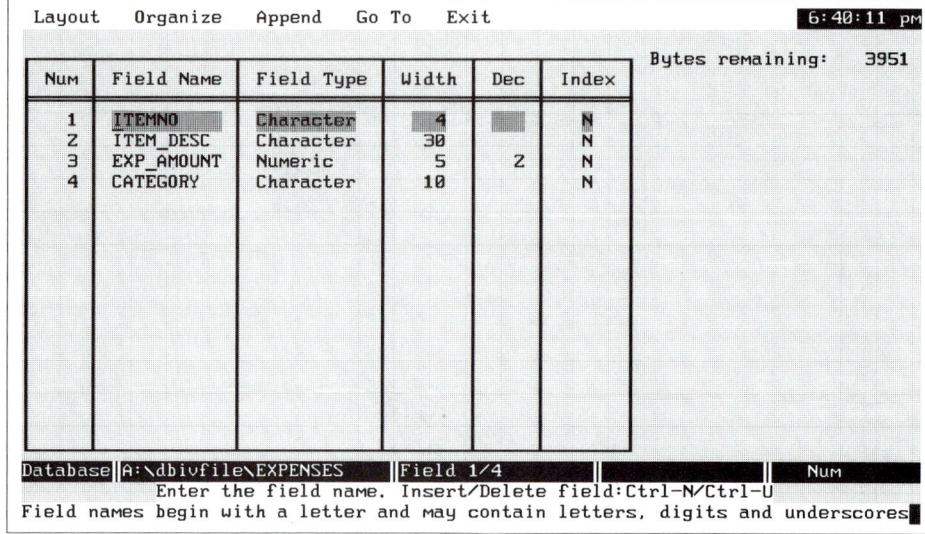

b. Add the records pictured in Figure 1.19 to the EXPENSES
   database.
c. Use Browse mode to display all the records and fields in the
   EXPENSES database.
d. Print a listing of the EXPENSES database.

Figure 1.19

The EXPENSES
database rec-
ords

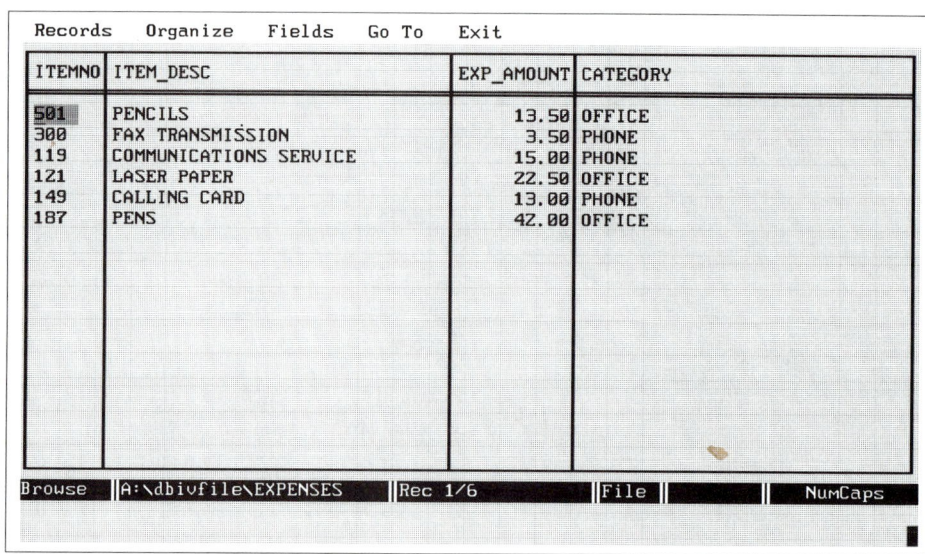

4. To practice modifying a database structure, perform the following tasks:
   a. Use the EXP-DATA database.
   b. Modify the structure of the EXP-DATA database by changing the width of the ITEM-DESC field from a width of 30 to a width of 25.
   c. Save the modified structure.
   d. Print the structure of the EXP-DATA database.

5. To practice using the Edit and Browse modes to edit a database, perform the following steps:
   a. Set up the INV-DATA database.
   b. Use Edit mode to view the record describing BATTERIES on the screen.
   c. Change the INSTOCK value from 25 to 15. Then change the SUPPLIER name from PARNELL to your last name. When finished, make sure to save your changes.
   d. Use Browse mode to view the INV-DATA database.
   e. Change the ORDERDATE fields for the following ITEMNO fields and then make sure to save your changes.

ITEMNO	ORDERDATE
209	5/19/89
289	4/21/89
399	6/16/89
405	7/13/89

   f. Print a listing of the INV-DATA database.

6. Create a database on the Advantage Diskette for storing the following list of books and then add the following data:
   - *How to Use dBASE IV*, Lori Pope, 0-89592-444-5, Waldorf Books, 1991
   - *Graphics—An Introduction*, Roger Carrera, 0-95263-331-7, Easy Book Publishers, 1990, 3rd Edition
   - *WordProcessing Fundamentals*, Johnson & Tremarchi, 0-33120-445-9, Waldorf Books, 1991
   - *Computers and You*, Ned Fernandez, 0-92611-333-7, University Press, 2nd Edition, 1991
   - *The Best of dBASE IV*, Lionel Siamette, 0-49921-220-7, University Press, 1990
   - *Programming Fundamentals*, John Yee and Julie Yee, 0-07-0324222-6, Easy Book Publishers, 1991, 5th Edition

---

MANAGING AND ORGANIZING DATA WITH dBASE IV

What if you want to delete a record from a database? Or change the contents of one or more records? Once you have entered data into a database, you need to know how to manage this valuable resource in order to keep it up to date. In addition, knowing how to rearrange the records in a database so they appear in a different order is critical to effective database management; viewing the database in a different order enables you to more clearly see the data stored in the database and make sense out of it.

PREVIEW

When you have completed this session, you will be able to:

Delete records from a database.
·
Index a database.
·
Create a single-field index.
·
Create a multiple-field index.
·
Sort a database.

WHY IS THIS SESSION IMPORTANT?

Now that you have learned how to create and add records to a database (Session 1), and to perform fundamental editing tasks, it is time to learn how to delete records from a database and to organize a database using the INDEX command and the SORT command. The tasks we lead you through in this session involve important—and commonly used—database management procedures.

Before proceeding, make sure the following are true:

1. You have loaded dBASE IV and are displaying the Control Center.

2. Your Advantage Diskette is inserted in the drive. You will save your work onto the diskette and retrieve the files that have been created for you. (*Note*: The Advantage Diskette can be made by copying all the files off the instructor's Master Advantage Diskette onto a formatted diskette.)

3. You have changed the current drive to the one that contains your Advantage Diskette. Remember that dBASE assumes the hard disk is the current drive until you change the drive. Refer to the section on Changing the Current Drive in Session1 if necessary.

DELETING A RECORD

Deleting a record from a database requires two steps: (1) mark the record for deletion and (2) permanently delete the marked record. One of the main reasons dBASE requires you to perform two steps to permanently delete a record is to protect you from accidentally deleting records with a single command. In this section, we lead you through deleting Joan Vieau's record because she has moved away.

MARKING A RECORD FOR DELETION

To mark a record for deletion you must be displaying the record you want to delete in either Edit or Browse mode.

To mark the record for deletion, do the following:

1. The Control Center should be displaying on the screen. Make the CUSTOMER database the active database by highlighting CUSTOMER in the Data panel, and then pressing (Enter). Then choose the Use file option. (This procedure was described in Session 1.)

2. Press (F2) until the data is displaying in Browse mode.

3. Use the cursor-movement keys to position the cursor on Joan Vieau's record.

4. To activate the Records menu:
    PRESS: (Alt)+R

5. Choose the Mark record for deletion option. "Del" should be displaying on the right side of the status line that is located on the bottom of the screen. "Del" indicates that Joan Vieau's record is now marked for deletion (Figure 2.1).

Figure 2.1

Marking a record for deletion. You know Joan Vieau's record is marked because "Del" displays when her record is highlighted.

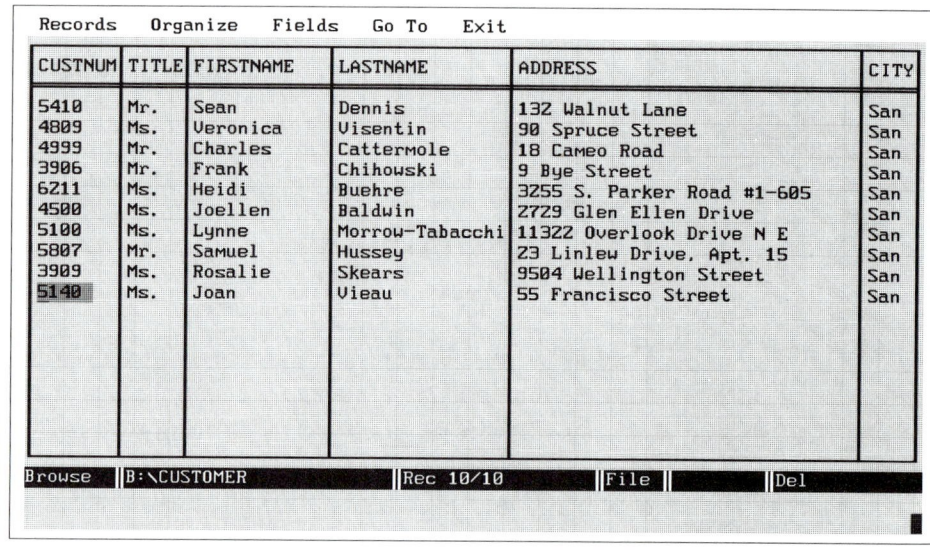

Quick Reference
Marking a
Record for
Deletion

1. Activate, or use, a database.
2. Press F2 to display the data in either Edit or Browse mode.
3. Position the cursor on the record you want to mark for deletion.
4. Activate the Records menu and choose the Mark record for deletion option.

DELETING A MARKED RECORD

To permanently delete a marked record, you must activate the Organize menu in either Edit or Browse mode. Perform the following steps:

1. You should be viewing the CUSTOMER database in either Edit or Browse mode; Joan Vieau's record has been marked for deletion.

2. To activate the Organize menu:
   TYPE: Alt+O

3. To permanently delete Joan Vieau's record, choose the Erase marked records option.

4. Choose the Yes option.
   Joan Vieau's record no longer appears in the database listing because it has been permanently deleted from the database.

5. To display the Control Center, choose the Exit option from the Exit menu.

Quick Reference
Deleting
Marked
Records

1. While displaying data in either Edit or Browse mode, activate the Organize menu.
2. Choose the Erase marked records option.
3. Choose the Yes option.

UNMARKING A RECORD MARKED FOR DELETION

To unmark a record that has been marked for deletion, you must activate the Records menu, and then highlight the record to be unmarked. The Mark record for deletion option toggles to display Clear deletion mark when the cursor is highlighting a marked record. If more than one record has been marked for deletion and you want to unmark them all at once, you must choose the Unmark all records option from the Organize menu.

Quick Reference   1. Display the data in either Edit or Browse mode.
Unmarking   2. Highlight the record you want to unmark.
a Record   3. Activate the Records menu, and then choose the Clear deletion mark option.

Quick Reference   1. Display the data in either Edit or Browse mode.
Unmarking   2. Choose the Unmark all records option from the Organize menu.
All Records

INDEXING THE DATABASE

Index files enable you to display database records in a different order without changing the physical location of the records in the database. Compared to *sorting* database records into a particular order, indexing provides the user with a number of advantages. The most significant advantage of **indexing** database records into order over sorting them is that indexing doesn't make an entire copy of the database, which can use up a tremendous amount of disk space if the database is large. Instead, indexing outputs an index file that contains pointers that determine the order of the database records. In addition, when records are added to a file that has been indexed into order, even the newly added records will appear in the correct positions when the database is displayed. When you add a record to a file that has been sorted, the record will always appear at the end of the database listing.

ABOUT INDEXING

You can index the records in a database file into many different orders. For example, you might sometimes want to view the database records in order by the LASTNAME field and at other times by the CITY field. When you *first* initiate a command to index a database into order, dBASE creates a **master index file** that has the same filename as the currently active database, plus an extension of MDX. If, for example, you create an index file to be used with the CUSTOMER database, dBASE would create a master file called CUSTOMER.MDX. When you then create an index to put the database into LASTNAME order, dBASE puts this specification, called a **tag**, into the associated MDX file. You can have up to 47 tags in an MDX file. Every time you add a record to, or delete a record from, the database file, all the tags in the associated MDX file are automatically updated, which can slow down processing if the MDX file contains many tags; therefore it isn't a good idea to create index tags you won't use. After creating a few index tags, you must use the Organize menu to tell dBASE which tag you want to activate.

Not only can you create index tags that are based on one field, but you can also create tags that are based on multiple fields. A **single-field index** is an index that puts database records into order by a single field. For example, you could create a single-field index to put the CUSTOMER database in order by the CITY field. But what if you want all the records within each city to be in order by another field, such as the LASTNAME field? You could accomplish this using a **multiple-field index**.

The process of creating an index file includes the following steps:

1. Initiate the Organize menu from the Edit or Browse screen.

2. Name the index tag.

3. Define the index expression (that is, the field you want to order the database by).

4. Define the order of the index tag (that is, ascending or descending).

5. Save, and then use, the index tag.

CREATING A SINGLE-FIELD INDEX

The next few steps will show you how to put the CUSTOMER database file into order by the CITY field.

Perform the following steps:

1. Make sure the CUSTOMER database is the active database.

2. The cursor should be highlighting CUSTOMER in the Control Center. To display the CUSTOMER database in either Edit or Browse mode:
   PRESS: F2

3. To display the Organize menu:
   PRESS: Alt + O

4. Choose the Create new index option. The screen should look like Figure 2.2.

Figure 2.2

Creating a new index

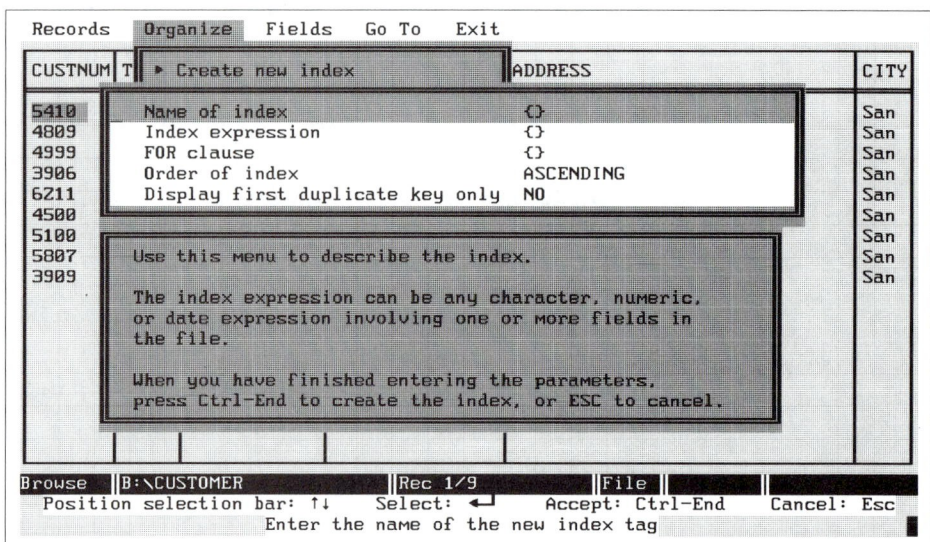

5. To specify a name for the index tag, press Enter to choose the Name of index option.

6. Type the following name for the index tag (*it's a good idea to name the tag with the same name as the field(s) you're ordering the database by*):
   TYPE: CITY
   PRESS: Enter

7. Choose the Index expression option by pressing Enter.

8. dBASE now wants to know what field you want to order the index by. *To enter a field expression, you can either type in the field name directly, or you can choose the field name from a field list using the EXPRESSION BUILDER command. The latter approach will often*

save time. As indicated on the bottom of the screen, you issue the EXPRESSION BUILDER command by pressing (Shift)+(F1). To pick a field name:

PRESS: (Shift)+(F1)

The screen should look like Figure 2.3.

Figure 2.3

Defining the field expression. Using the (Shift)+(F1) command, you can pick the field expression from a field list.

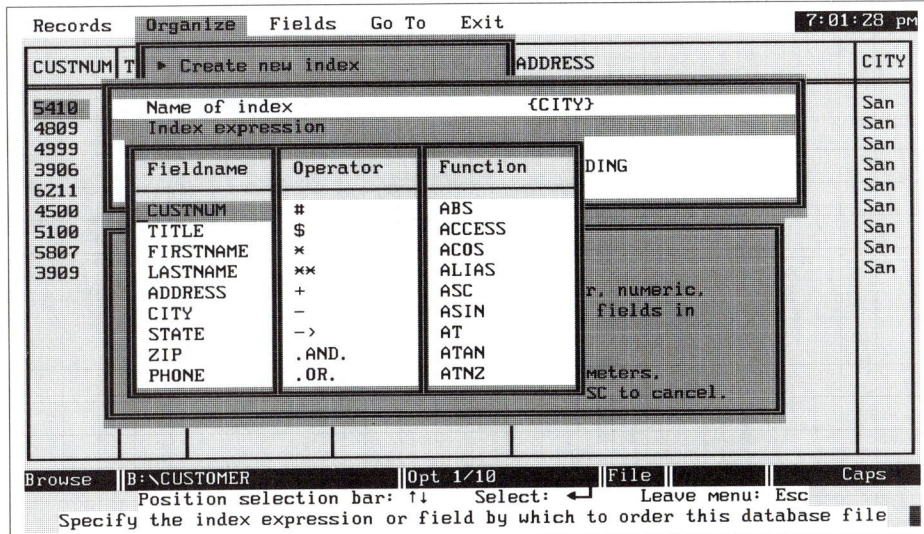

9. Since you want the database to be listed in order by the CITY field, highlight the CITY field and then press (Enter). The name CITY should be displaying as the Index Expression.

10. To tell dBASE you're finished defining the index expression:
    PRESS: (Enter)

11. Since you're now finished defining the index:
    PRESS: (Ctrl)+(End)

12. If you press (Tab) a few times to see the CITY field, the screen should look similar to Figure 2.4. Note that the records are displaying in order by the CITY field.

Figure 2.4

The CUSTOMER database has been indexed into order by the CITY field.

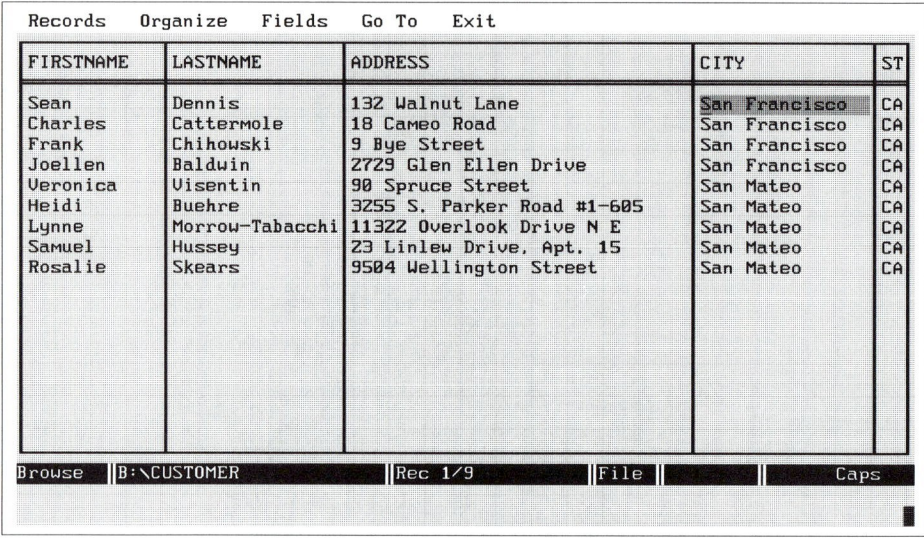

```
  Records   Organize   Fields   Go To   Exit

 FIRSTNAME   LASTNAME         ADDRESS                      CITY            ST

 Sean        Dennis           132 Walnut Lane              San Francisco   CA
 Charles     Cattermole       18 Cameo Road                San Francisco   CA
 Frank       Chihowski        9 Bye Street                 San Francisco   CA
 Joellen     Balduin          2729 Glen Ellen Drive        San Francisco   CA
 Veronica    Visentin         90 Spruce Street             San Mateo       CA
 Heidi       Buehre           3255 S. Parker Road #1-605   San Mateo       CA
 Lynne       Morrow-Tabacchi  11322 Overlook Drive N E     San Mateo       CA
 Samuel      Hussey           23 Linlew Drive, Apt. 15     San Mateo       CA
 Rosalie     Skears           9504 Wellington Street       San Mateo       CA




 Browse   ║B:\CUSTOMER               ║Rec 1/9        ║File ║        ║        Caps
```

13. To display the Control Center:
    PRESS: (Esc)

....

Quick Reference
Creating an
Index

1. Activate, or use, a database.
2. Press (F2) to display the data in either Edit mode or Browse mode.
3. Activate the Organize menu and choose the Create new index option.
4. Choose the Name of index option, type a name for the index, and then press (Enter).
5. Choose the Index expression option.
6. Type in the field name you want to index on and then press (Enter); or press (Shift)+(F1) to choose a name from a field list, and then press (Enter).

....

USING AN INDEX

When you create an index, your data is automatically displayed in order according to the new index. To use a different index (if you have more than one index tag in an MDX file), choose the Order records by index option from the Organize menu. A list of the index tags for the current database will display. Choose the index you want to use to order the database.

....

Quick Reference 1. While displaying a database in either Edit or Browse mode, choose
Using an   the Order records by index option from the Organize menu.
Index   2. Choose the index you want to use to order the database.

....

CREATING A MULTIPLE-FIELD INDEX

The steps for creating a multiple-field index are identical to those for creating a single-field index except that more than one field is referenced in the index expression. The CITY index you created earlier puts the CUSTOMER database into order by the CITY field. The records for each city, however, aren't in any particular order. As described earlier, an example of when you might want to create a multiple-field index would be if you want to display the database in CITY order and all the records for each city in LASTNAME order. In this case, the index expression in the index tag would look like the following:
CITY+LASTNAME

If your database contains people who have the same last name, which is extremely likely, you may want your index expression to be the following:
CITY+LASTNAME+FIRSTNAME

To create an index called CITY1 that will put the CUSTOMER database into CITY order and then into LASTNAME order, perform the following steps:

1. Make sure the CUSTOMER database is the active database.

2. The cursor should be highlighting CUSTOMER in the Control Center. To display the CUSTOMER database in either Edit or Browse mode:
    PRESS: F2

3. To display the Organize menu:
    PRESS: Alt+O

4. Choose the Create new index option.

5. To specify a name for the index tag, press Enter to choose the Name of index option.

6. Type the following name for the index tag:
    TYPE: CITY1
    PRESS: (Enter)

7. Choose the Index expression option by pressing (Enter).

8. Since you want the database to be listed in order by the CITY and
    LASTNAME fields:
    TYPE: CITY+LASTNAME
    PRESS: (Enter)
    (*Note*: You could have chosen the fields from a field list using
    (Shift)+(F1).) The screen should look like Figure 2.5.

Figure 2.5

Multiple-field
index. To create
a multiple-field
index, you must
separate each
field in the field
expression with
a plus (+) sign.

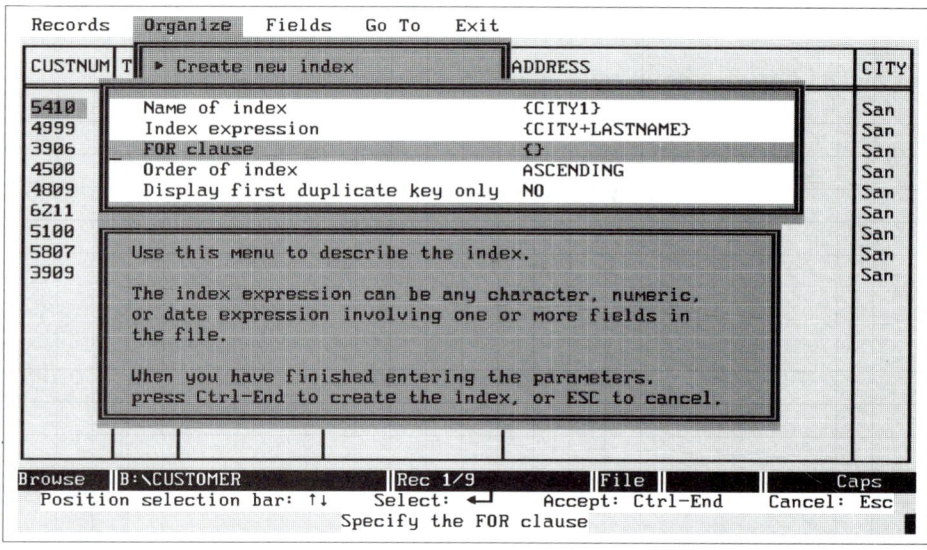

```
  Records   Organize   Fields   Go To   Exit

 CUSTNUM T   ► Create new index              ADDRESS              CITY
 ┌──────────────────────────────────────────────────────────────┐
 5410        Name of index             {CITY1}                    San
 4999        Index expression          {CITY+LASTNAME}            San
 3906        FOR clause                {}                         San
 4500        Order of index            ASCENDING                  San
 4809        Display first duplicate key only  NO                 San
 6211                                                             San
 5100                                                             San
 5807        Use this menu to describe the index.                San
 3909                                                             San
             The index expression can be any character, numeric,
             or date expression involving one or more fields in
             the file.

             When you have finished entering the parameters,
             press Ctrl-End to create the index, or ESC to cancel.


 Browse  ║B:\CUSTOMER          ║Rec 1/9        ║File ║          Caps
   Position selection bar: ↑↓      Select: ◄┘    Accept: Ctrl-End   Cancel: Esc
                           Specify the FOR clause
```

---

9. Since you're now finished defining the index:
    PRESS: (Ctrl)+(End)

10. After you press (Tab) a few times, the screen should look similar to
    Figure 2.6. Note that the records for each city are displayed in order by
    the LASTNAME field.

11. To display the Control Center:
    PRESS: (Esc)

Figure 2.6

The CUSTOMER database has been indexed into order by the CITY field; for each city, the records are in LASTNAME order.

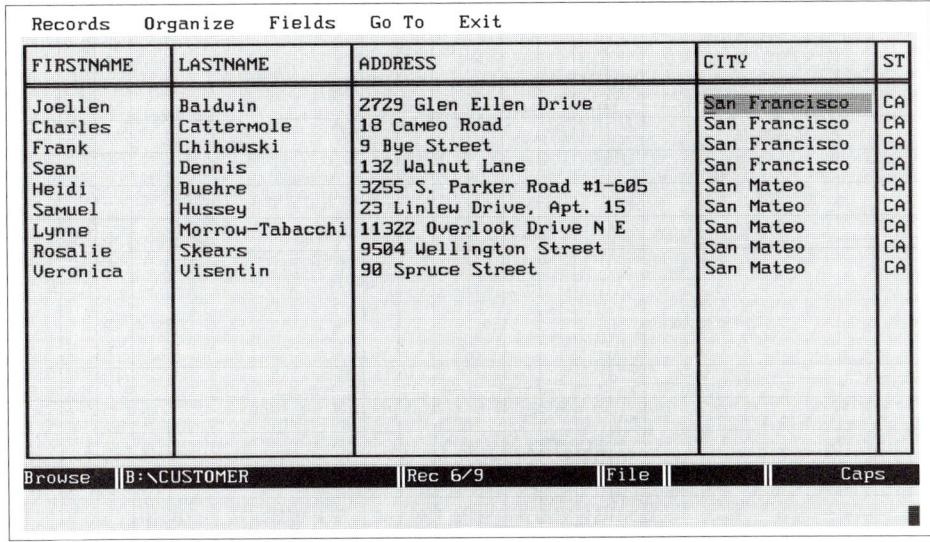

```
  Records   Organize   Fields   Go To   Exit

  FIRSTNAME    LASTNAME        ADDRESS                     CITY           ST

  Joellen      Balduin         2729 Glen Ellen Drive       San Francisco  CA
  Charles      Cattermole      18 Cameo Road               San Francisco  CA
  Frank        Chihowski       9 Bye Street                San Francisco  CA
  Sean         Dennis          132 Walnut Lane             San Francisco  CA
  Heidi        Buehre          3255 S. Parker Road #1-605   San Mateo      CA
  Samuel       Hussey          23 Linlew Drive, Apt. 15    San Mateo      CA
  Lynne        Morrow-Tabacchi 11322 Overlook Drive N E    San Mateo      CA
  Rosalie      Skears          9504 Wellington Street      San Mateo      CA
  Veronica     Visentin        90 Spruce Street            San Mateo      CA




  Browse    B:\CUSTOMER               Rec 6/9        File              Caps
```

MODIFYING AN INDEX

There may be times when you want to modify an existing index. For example, instead of creating a new index called CITY1 to put the CUSTOMER database into order by the CITY field, and all the records for each city into order by the LASTNAME field, you could have modified the CITY index. To modify an index, you must choose the Modify existing index option from the Organize menu. A list of the index tags in the active MDX file will list on the screen. Choose the index tag you want to modify by highlighting it and then pressing (Enter). After making changes to the index expression, save your changes by pressing (Ctrl)+(End).

Quick Reference
Modifying
an Index

1. Display the data in either Edit or Browse mode.
2. From the Organize menu, choose the Modify existing index option.
3. Choose the index tag you want to modify by highlighting it and then pressing (Enter).
4. After making changes to the index expression, save your changes by pressing (Ctrl)+(End).

HIDING DUPLICATE RECORDS

In most cases, you will want to see every record in a database. However, if you are working with an employee database, for example, you may want to just list the unique hourly wage amounts plus the associated hire dates. Or you may want to list each existing combination of job title plus salary. Once a record containing a certain combination is listed, all other records with that combination are to be "hidden," that is, not included in the listing. To modify an index to hide duplicate records, you must choose the Modify existing index option from the Organize menu. Highlight the index you want to modify and press [Enter] to choose the index. Choose the Display first duplicate key only option and press [Enter] to change the setting to Yes. To save the modified index, press [Ctrl]+[End].

Quick Reference
Hiding
Duplicate
Records

1. Display the data in either Edit or Browse mode.
2. To modify an index to hide duplicate records, you must choose the Modify existing index option from the Organize menu.
3. Highlight the index you want to modify and press [Enter] to choose the index.
4. Choose the Display first duplicate key only option and press [Enter] to change the setting to Yes.
5. To save the modified index:
   PRESS: [Ctrl]+[End]

REMOVING AN INDEX

dBASE automatically updates all indexes in the open MDX file when you make changes to the current database. To improve processing speed, you should remove any indexes you don't need. To remove an index, choose the Remove unwanted index tag option from the Organize menu. A list of index tags will display. Choose the index tag you want to delete by highlighting it and pressing [Enter]. The index tag is removed from the MDX file.

In this section you will remove the CITY index tag, because the CITY1 index tag is more useful. (You created the CITY1 index in the Creating a Multiple-Field Index section.) Perform the following steps:

1. Display the CUSTOMER database in either Edit or Browse mode.

2. Choose the Remove unwanted index tag from the Organize menu. A list of indexes should be displaying on the right side of the screen.

3. Highlight the CITY index and press [Enter]. The index tag has now been removed from the database.

4. To display the Control Center:
   PRESS: (Esc) *twice*

Quick Reference
*Removing
an Index*

1. Display the data in either Edit or Browse mode.
2. Choose the Remove unwanted index tag option from the Organize menu.
3. Choose the index tag you want to delete by highlighting it and pressing (Enter).

SORTING THE DATABASE

In this section you will use the SORT command to put the CUSTOMER database into order by the CUSTNUM field. **Sorting** a database creates a new file that contains an entire copy of your database in sorted order. Creating a copy can be a problem if your database contains over 1,000 records and you are getting short of disk space! However, the SORT command can do one thing that the INDEX command cannot. The SORT command lets you do an ascending sort on one field and a descending sort on another at the same time. You cannot do this with a multiple-field index. Another reason you may want to sort a database file rather than index it is if you know the database file will never change.

Perform the following steps to sort the CUSTOMER database into CUSTNUM order:

1. The Control Center should be displaying on the screen. Highlight CUSTOMER and then press (F2) to display the data in either Edit or Browse mode.

2. To display the Organize menu:
   PRESS: (Alt)+O

3. Choose the Sort database on field list option.

4. dBASE is now waiting for you to type in the name of the field you want to sort on. You can either type the field name in directly or pick a field from a field list.

To pick a field from a field list:
PRESS: (Shift)+(F1)
The screen should look like Figure 2.7.

Figure 2.7

Sorting the CUS-
TOMER database.
After giving the
SORT command,
use (Shift)+(F1)
to display a list of
filenames.

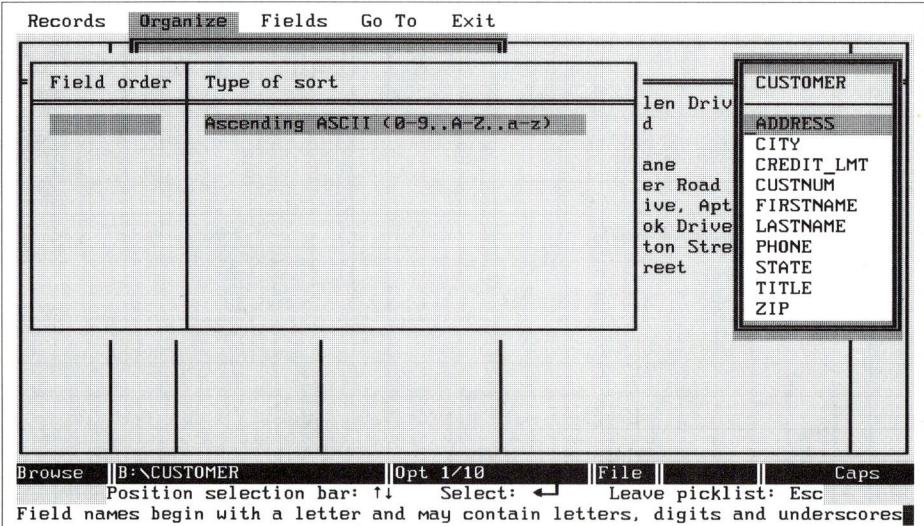

5. Choose the CUSTNUM field by highlighting it and then pressing
   (Enter). CUSTNUM should now appear in the "Field order" column.

6. To move the cursor to the "Type of sort" column:
   PRESS: (Enter)
   Note: dBASE lets you perform four types of sorts. These sorts are
   listed in Table 2.1. A **dictionary sort** isn't sensitive to case. Therefore,
   if you choose "Ascending dictionary," all the records that begin with
   either *a* or *A* will be listed before records that begin with *b* or *B*. **ASCII
   sorts** are sensitive to case. Uppercase letters will always come before
   lowercase letters. Therefore, if you choose "Ascending ASCII," *Zebra*
   will come before *apple*.

7. Because the CUSTNUM field is a character field that contains
   numbers, it doesn't matter whether you choose ASCII or dictionary as
   the sort type. The current assumption of "Ascending ASCII" is fine.
   (*Note*: To change the sort type, press the Space Bar while the cursor is
   in the "Type of sort" column.)

Table 2.1	Name	Example	Purpose
Different Sort Types	Ascending ASCII	0...9, A...Z, a...z	The sort will be case sensitive.
	Descending ASCII	z...a, Z...A, 9...0	The sort will be case sensitive.
	Ascending Dictionary	0...9, Aa...Zz	The sort won't be case sensitive.
	Descending Dictionary	zZ...aA, 9...0	The sort won't be case sensitive.

8. To sort the CUSTOMER database, you must issue the command to save the sort specifications:
PRESS: [Ctrl]+[End]

9. dBASE now wants you to name the newly sorted file. You will name the sorted file CUSTNUM.
TYPE: CUSTNUM
PRESS: [Enter]

10. If you want, you can now type a description for the sorted file. After typing a description, press [Enter].

11. The CUSTOMER database is still in its original order. A copy of the CUSTOMER database, called CUSTNUM, has been made that is in CUSTNUM order. You must make the CUSTNUM database the active database in order to see the records in ascending order by the CUSTNUM field.
   a. Press [Esc] to display the Control Center.
   b. Highlight CUSTNUM in the Data panel, and press [Enter]. Then choose the Use file option.
   c. Press [F2] until the data is displayed in Browse mode. The data should be listed in order by the CUSTNUM field.
   d. Press [Esc] to display the Control Center.

Quick Reference
Sorting a
Database

1. Display the data in either Edit or Browse mode.
2. Choose the Sort database on field list option from the Organize menu.
3. At this point, you can either type the name of the field on which you want to sort or pick a field from a field list by pressing [Shift]+[F1].
4. To move the cursor to the Type of sort column, press [Enter]. Press the Space Bar to display the appropriate sort type.
5. To execute the sort:
   PRESS: [Ctrl]+[End]
6. Type a name for the newly sorted file and press [Enter]. Then type an optional description for the sorted file and press [Enter].

SUMMARY

In this session you learned how to delete records from a database using the Organize menu that displays when you view your database in either Edit or Browse mode. To delete a record, you must first mark the record for deletion and then use a different command to erase the marked record. After marking a record, dBASE provides you with a command to unmark a record if you decide that you don't want the record erased after all.

You also learned how to create single- and multiple-field indexes, which enable you to display a database in a different order. To create an index you must use the Organize menu that is available to you when you display the database in either Edit or Browse mode. Creating an index involves choosing the field(s) by which you want to order the database. Once you've created one or more indexes, choose the appropriate index using the Order records by index option of the Organize menu.

Indexing a database is generally preferable to sorting a database because the SORT command creates an entire copy of the original database in sorted order, which takes up valuable disk space.

COMMAND SUMMARY

The table on the following pages provides a list of the commands and procedures covered in this session.

Table 2.2 Command Summary	Marking a Record for Deletion	1. Activate, or use, a database. 2. Press F2 to display the data in either Edit or Browse mode. 3. Position the cursor on the record you want to mark for deletion. 4. Activate the Records menu and choose the Mark record for deletion option.
	Deleting Marked Records	1. While displaying data in either Edit or Browse mode, activate the Organize menu. 2. Choose the Erase marked records option. 3. Choose the Yes option.
	Unmarking a Record	1. Display the data in either Edit or Browse mode. 2. Highlight the record you want to unmark. 3. Activate the Records menu, and then choose the Clear deletion mark option.
	Unmarking all Records	1. Display the data in either Edit or Browse mode. 2. Choose the Unmark all records option from the Organize menu.
	Creating an Index	1. Activate, or use, a database. 2. Press F2 to display the data in either Edit mode or Browse mode. 3. Activate the Organize menu and choose the Create new index option. 4. Choose the Name of index option, type a name for the index, and then press Enter. 5. Choose the Index expression option. 6. Type in the field name you want to index on and then press Enter; or press Shift+F1 to choose a name from a field list, and then press Enter.

Table 2.2 Command Summary (continued)	Using an Index	1. While displaying a database in either Edit or Browse mode, choose the Order records by index option from the Organize menu. 2. Choose the index you want to use to order the database.
	Modifying an Index	1. Display the data in either Edit or Browse mode. 2. From the Organize menu, choose the Modify existing index option. 3. Choose the index tag you want to modify by highlighting it and then pressing Enter. 4. After making changes to the index expression, save your changes by pressing Ctrl+End.
	Hiding Duplicate Records	1. Display the data in either Edit or Browse mode. 2. To modify an index to hide duplicate records, you must choose the Modify existing index option from the Organize menu. 3. Highlight the index you want to modify and press to choose the index. 4. Choose the Display first duplicate key only option and press Enter to change the setting to Yes. 5. To save the modified index: PRESS: Ctrl+End
	Removing an Index	1. Display the data in either Edit or Browse mode. 2. Choose the Remove unwanted index tag option from the Organize menu. 3. Choose the index tag you want to delete by highlighting it and pressing Enter.

Table 2.2	Sorting a Database	1. Display the data in either Edit or Browse mode.
Command Summary (concluded)		2. Choose the Sort database on field list option from the Organize menu.
		3. At this point, you can either type the name of the field on which you want to sort or pick a field from a field list by pressing Shift+F1.
		4. To move the cursor to the Type of sort column, press Enter. Press the Space Bar to display the appropriate sort type.
		5. To execute the sort: PRESS: Ctrl+End
		6. Type a name in for the newly sorted file and press Enter. Then type an optional description in for the sorted file and press Enter.

KEY TERMS

ASCII sort   A dBASE IV sort that is case sensitive (sorts all capitalized entries apart from all lowercase entries).

dictionary sort   A dBASE IV sort that isn't case sensitive.

indexing   Process of creating or using an index.

master index file   In dBASE IV, when the user first initiates a command to index a database into order, dBASE creates this file, which has the same filename as the currently active database, plus an extension of MDX.

multiple-field index   A dBASE IV index based on more than one field.

single-field index   A dBASE IV index that is based on one field.

sorting   Process of reorganizing a database into a different order.

tag   Specification stored in a master index file that determines the order
of the database.

EXERCISES

SHORT ANSWER

1. To permanently remove a record from a database, what two commands must you use?
2. When compared to indexing, what is the main disadvantage of sorting a database into order?
3. After you have marked a record for deletion, what must you do if you decide you don't want to remove the record from the database after all?
4. Provide an example of when you might want to create a multiple-field index.
5. After sorting a database into order (as opposed to indexing), what must you do in order to view the sorted file?
6. What advantages does indexing a database provide over sorting a database?
7. What is an index tag?
8. Why is it often necessary to change the current disk drive using dBASE IV?
9. What is the purpose of a dBASE IV file that has an extension of MDX?
10. Provide an example of when you might want to create an index that hides duplicate records.

HANDS-ON

1. To practice marking records for deletion, unmarking a record, and deleting a marked record, perform the following steps:
   a. Set up the EXP-DATA database.
   b. Mark the record describing the Pencils expense for deletion.
   c. Mark the record describing the Laser Paper expense for deletion.
   d. Unmark the record describing the Pencils expense.
   e. Permanently delete the Laser Paper expense record.
   f. Print a list of all the records and fields in the EXP-DATA database.

2. To practice creating indexes, make the INVOICE database the active database and then perform the following steps:

   a. Create an index that will put this database into order by the ITEMNAME field. Name the index INVOICE1.

   b. Create an index that will put the database into order by the ITEMNAME field, and for each ITEMNAME the records should be in order by the INVNUM field. Name the index INVOICE2.

   c. Print a listing of all the records and fields stored in the INVOICE database.

3. To practice creating and modifying an index, perform the following steps using the EMP-DATA database:

   a. Create an index tag that will put this database into order by the CITY field. Name the index CITY.

   b. Modify the CITY index so that it will not only put the database into order by the CITY field, but for each city the records will be in order by the LASTNAME field.

4. To practice indexing a database, make the SUPPLIER database the active database and then perform the following steps:

   a. Create a single-field index to put the SUPPLIER database into order by the SUPPLIER field. Name the index SUPP1.

   b. Create a multiple-field index to put the SUPPLIER database into order by the SUPPLIER field and the COMPANY field. Name the index SUPP2.

   c. Print a listing of the SUPPLIER database. *Note*: Since the database is too wide to fit on the page, only the first four fields will list.

SESSION 3

QUERIES

What use would a database be if you couldn't ask questions of it? For example, how many customers live in San Francisco? How many customers live in either San Mateo or San Francisco? How many owe us more than $500? This session shows you how to use the Query group of commands so you can retrieve the information you need from your database.

PREVIEW

When you have completed this session, you will be able to:

Retrieve information from your database.

Organize the information you retrieve from a database.

View specific database records that meet your criteria.

Why Is This Session Important?
The Queries Design Screen and Moving the
  Cursor
The Fundamentals of Creating Views
      Removing Fields from a View
      Adding Fields to a View
      Removing and Adding All Fields
      Displaying and Printing the View
        Data
      Moving Fields
      Renaming View Fields
      Saving and Describing View Queries
Organizing View Records
      Organizing Without an Index
      About Organizing with an Index
      Determining Which Fields Have an
        Associated Index
      Organizing on a Single-Field Index
      Organizing on a Multiple-Field Index
Adding a Calculated Field in a View
Searching a Database
Summary
      Command Summary
Key Terms
Exercises
      Short Answer
      Hands-On

WHY IS THIS SESSION IMPORTANT?

dBASE IV provides a variety of commands that enable you to view specific fields and records that are stored in a database. Each of these commands involves using the Queries panel from the Control Center. In the next few sections you learn how to create view queries to display data stored in the CUSTOMER database. A **view query** provides the user with a view, or partial picture, of the data stored in a database file. The basic steps for creating and using view queries are:

1. Use, or open, a database file.

2. Decide what fields to display in the view.

3. Decide what records to display in the view.

4. Display the data (F2).

5. Name and save the view query (optional).

As we will describe in this session, creating a view query can involve many more steps, depending on your needs. In this session you learn how to take control of your database by retrieving the information you need to make business decisions.

Before proceeding, make sure the following are true:

1. You have loaded dBASE IV and are displaying the Control Center.

2. Your Advantage Diskette is inserted in the drive. You will save your work onto the diskette and retrieve the files that have been created for you. (*Note*: The Advantage Diskette can be made by copying all the files off the instructor's Master Advantage Diskette onto a formatted diskette.)

3. You have changed the current drive to the one that contains your Advantage Diskette. Remember that dBASE assumes the hard disk is the current drive until you change the drive. Refer to the section on Changing the Current Drive in Session1 if necessary.

THE QUERIES DESIGN SCREEN AND MOVING THE CURSOR

In this section we describe the different components of the Queries design screen and lead you through navigating the cursor around it. You will then use the Queries design screen to view all the fields and records in the CUSTOMER database.

1. Make sure the CUSTOMER database has been set up for use and that you are viewing the Control Center.

2. Highlight the <create> marker in the Queries panel, and then press `Enter`.

The screen should look like Figure 3.1. You are now viewing the Queries design screen. Across the top of the screen is the menu bar with options for tailoring a database view to your needs. Below the menu bar is the **file skeleton**, or graphic representation of the active database file showing the names of all the fields in the database. The name of the active database (CUSTOMER.DBF) is displayed on the left of the file skeleton; the field names are listed to the right. As you will learn in this session, in the Filtering Data section, you can type selection criteria into the space below each of the field names in order to be selective about the records that are listed on the screen. You will also learn that you can use up to eight file skeletons on one Queries design screen.

Note that an arrow automatically precedes each field name. An arrow before a field name causes that field to be displayed when you view the database data. At this point all fields will be displayed because they are all preceded by arrows. Displaying on the bottom of the screen is the format for the current view of the data, called the **view skeleton**. The right arrow in the bottom right-hand corner of the view box indicates that more fields are included in the view than can currently fit on the screen.

Figure 3.1

The Queries design screen. The file skeleton is displaying on the top of the screen; the view skeleton is displaying on the bottom of the screen.

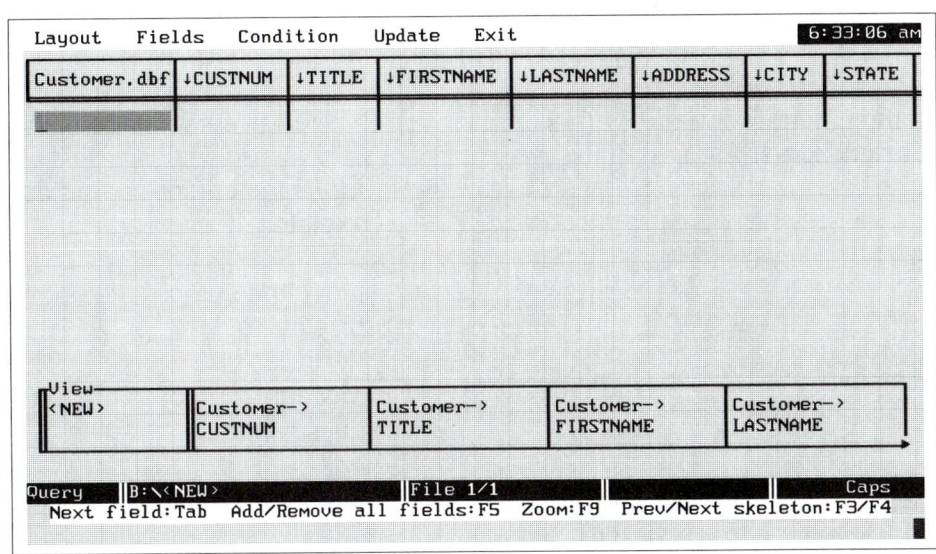

```
Layout   Fields   Condition   Update   Exit                    6:33:06 am
 Customer.dbf ↓CUSTNUM  ↓TITLE  ↓FIRSTNAME  ↓LASTNAME  ↓ADDRESS  ↓CITY  ↓STATE
 ██████████



 View
 <NEW>        Customer->    Customer->    Customer->    Customer->
              CUSTNUM       TITLE         FIRSTNAME     LASTNAME
 Query    B:\<NEW>              File 1/1                            Caps
    Next field:Tab   Add/Remove all fields:F5   Zoom:F9   Prev/Next skeleton:F3/F4
```

In the following steps we lead you through different methods of moving the cursor around the Queries design screen.

3. Note that you can't see all the fields on the screen.
   PRESS: (Tab)
   The cursor should be positioned beneath the CUSTNUM field.

4. PRESS: (Tab) *until you can see the CREDIT_LMT field on the screen*
   Note that the view on the bottom of the screen stayed the same.

5. To move the cursor to the view skeleton:
   PRESS: (F3)
   The cursor should now be highlighting the first field in the view skeleton.
   PRESS: (Tab) *until you see the CREDIT_LMT field*
   When you move fields, later in this session, you will need to move the cursor into the view skeleton.

6. To move the cursor back to the top of the screen, away from the view skeleton:
   PRESS: (F3)

7. The cursor should be positioned on the top of the screen. To move the cursor back to the TITLE field:
   PRESS: (Shift)+(Tab) *until the cursor is beneath "Customer.dbf".*
   Table 3.1 lists a few different methods for moving the cursor in the Queries design screen.

Table 3.1	⬚ Prev, ⬚ Next	Move between the file and view skeletons and the condition boxes
Moving the cursor in the Queries Design Screen	⬚, ⬚	Move the cursor within a column
	⬚, ⬚	Move the cursor up and down within the file skeleton
	⬚	Move the cursor to the right when columns are displaying
	⬚+⬚	Move the cursor to the left when columns are displaying
	⬚	Move the cursor to the right most column
	⬚	Move the cursor to the left most column
	⬚	Display the next group of file skeletons (when you have more than can fit on the screen)
	⬚	Display the previous group of file skeletons

8. To view all the records and fields stored in the CUSTOMER database:
   PRESS: F2 *until the data is displaying in Browse mode*

9. In Browse mode, note that you can't see all the fields stored in the database.
   PRESS: Tab *to view the fields to the right*

10. To view the Queries design screen again:
    PRESS: Shift+F2

You will use the procedures described in this section frequently when using the Queries design screen.

THE FUNDAMENTALS OF CREATING VIEWS

In the next few sections you will learn important procedures to help you create view queries. You will learn how to remove fields from and add fields to your view of a database. In addition, you will learn how to move and rename the fields you use in a view. Once the view of your database looks the way you want, you will save your view specifications so you can use them again later.

REMOVING FIELDS FROM A VIEW

As described in the last section, when you first enter the Queries design screen, all fields are chosen to be included in the view; you know this because every field has an arrow next to it. If you want certain fields to be hidden from view, such as salary data that might be stored in an employee database, you can remove the field from view.

To practice removing fields from view, you will now remove the TITLE, FIRSTNAME, ADDRESS, and STATE fields from the view. Perform the following steps:

1. Position the cursor in the TITLE field of either the file or view skeleton. (Note: *When removing a field, your cursor can be highlighting the field in either the file or view skeleton.*)

2. To display the Fields menu:
   PRESS: Alt+F

3. The Remove field from view option should be highlighted. To choose this option:
   PRESS: Enter
   The arrow should have disappeared from the TITLE field.

4. A quick alternative to using the Fields menu to remove a field from a view is to use F5 (Field). Simply position the cursor in the field you want to remove from the view, and then press F5; the field will be removed. If you press F5 again, the field will be included again. Use this procedure to remove the FIRSTNAME, ADDRESS, and STATE fields from the view. Note that when you remove a field from the file skeleton, it is also removed from the view skeleton.

5. To see data in the current view:
   PRESS: F2
   Note that all the fields in the view can fit on the screen.

6. To display the Queries design screen:
   PRESS: Shift + F2

Quick Reference   1. Display the Queries design screen.
Removing a   2. Highlight the field you want to remove.
Field from a   3. Choose the Remove field from view option from the Fields menu, or
View   press F5.

ADDING FIELDS TO A VIEW

The procedure to add a field is almost identical to that of removing a field. Position the cursor in the field to be added; choose the Add field to view option from the Fields menu or press F5. To add all fields, position the cursor beneath the filename in the file skeleton and then press F5.

Quick Reference   1. Display the Queries design screen.
Adding a Field   2. Position the cursor in the field to be added.
to a View   3. Choose the Add field to view option from the Fields menu, or press
                              F5.

REMOVING AND ADDING ALL FIELDS

There may be times when you'll want to view only a few fields. In this case it may be easier to unmark all the fields at once and to then add the few fields to be included in the view (we describe adding fields in the next section). To remove all the fields at once, you must position the cursor beneath the filename in the file skeleton, and then press F5. When all fields are chosen in the file skeleton, F5 unmarks all fields; if a few fields, or no fields, are chosen in the file skeleton, F5 marks the rest of the fields.

To show you how to use F5, perform the following steps:

1. Position the cursor beneath the Customer.dbf filename in the file skeleton. At this point, since a few fields aren't chosen to be viewed, pressing F5 at this point will cause dBASE to choose the rest of the fields. Pressing F5 again will remove all the fields. To remove all fields from the view:
    PRESS: F5 *twice*
    Note that the view skeleton has disappeared since no fields are currently chosen to be viewed.

2. To add all fields to the view again:
    PRESS: F5
    Each field should again appear with an arrow next to it and the view skeleton should again be displaying on the bottom of the screen.

Quick Reference
Removing and
Adding All Fields
in a View

1. Display the Queries design screen.
2. Position the cursor beneath the filename in the file skeleton, and press F5 once or twice to remove or add all the fields in the view.

DISPLAYING AND PRINTING THE VIEW DATA

To display data while viewing the Queries design screen, press F2. If you want to print the displayed data, use the QUICK REPORT command (Shift+F9) and then choose the Begin printing option. *Note*: While displaying the data, you can make changes to, or edit, the data stored in the active database. To return to the Queries design screen, press Shift+F2.

When viewing the Control Center, highlight the name of the view query (you learn how to save view queries shortly) in the Queries panel and press F2. View queries are given the extension of QBE.

Quick Reference
*Displaying and
Printing the
View Data*

While viewing the Queries design screen:
1. Press F2 to display your data. At this point, if necessary, you can edit the data viewed. You can print the displayed data by pressing Shift+F9 and then choosing the Begin printing option.
2. To return to the Queries design screen, press Shift+F2.

While viewing the Control Center:
Highlight the view file in the Queries panel (view files have the extension of QBE) and press F2.

MOVING FIELDS

Unless you move the fields in your view, they are listed in the order in which they were defined in the database structure. There may be times that you want the fields in your database to be listed in a different order. For example, you may want the CUSTNUM field in the CUSTOMER database to be listed last so that the customer's name information is listed first for easy reference.

In this section we lead you through moving the CUSTNUM field so it is listed last in the view:

1. First remove the TITLE, ADDRESS, STATE, and ZIP fields from the view (follow the steps for removing fields as described in this session) so that fewer fields are listing.

2. To move the CUSTNUM field so it is listed last, you must first position the cursor in the view skeleton.
   PRESS: F3

3. The cursor should be highlighting the CUSTNUM field in the view skeleton.

4. To select a field to be moved, as indicated on the bottom of the screen, use F6 (Select).
   PRESS: F6
   The screen should look like Figure 3.2. *At this point, if you want to select more fields to be moved, press Tab or Shift+Tab. If you want to unselect a field, press Esc.*

Figure 3.2

The CUSTNUM field, in the view skeleton, has been selected (using `F6`) to be moved.

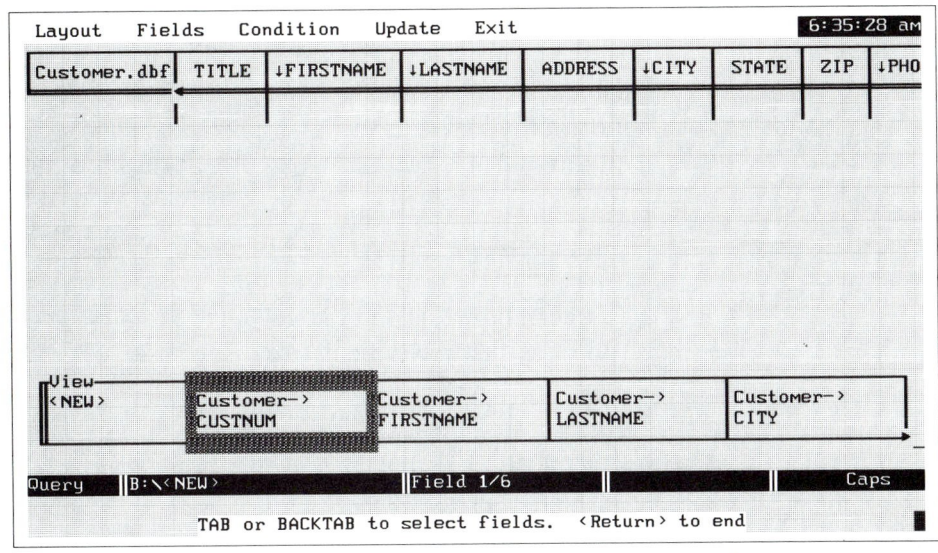

```
 Layout   Fields   Condition   Update   Exit                    6:35:28 am
┌──────────┬───────┬───────────┬──────────┬─────────┬───────┬───────┬──────┐
│Customer.dbf│ TITLE │↓FIRSTNAME │↓LASTNAME │ ADDRESS │↓CITY  │ STATE │ ZIP │↓PHO│
└──────────┴───────┴───────────┴──────────┴─────────┴───────┴───────┴──────┘



 ┌View─────┬──────────┬──────────┬──────────┬──────────┐
 │<NEW>    │Customer─>│Customer─>│Customer─>│Customer─>│
 │         │CUSTNUM   │FIRSTNAME │LASTNAME  │CITY      │
 └─────────┴──────────┴──────────┴──────────┴──────────┘
 Query  B:\<NEW>              Field 1/6                          Caps
              TAB or BACKTAB to select fields.   <Return> to end
```

5. To finish selecting the field(s) you want to move:
   PRESS: `Enter`

6. To move the selected field, you must press `F7` (Move), move the cursor to where the field should be positioned, and then press `Enter`. To initiate the MOVE command:
   PRESS: `F7`
   To move the field so it is positioned last in the listing:
   PRESS: `Tab` *until the cursor is positioned after CREDIT_LMT*
   PRESS: `Enter`

7. To view the data:
   PRESS: `F2`
   The CUSTNUM field should be displaying on the right side of the screen.

....

Quick Reference
Moving
Fields

1. Display the Queries design screen.
2. Press `F3` to position the cursor in the view skeleton.
3. Highlight the field you want to move, and then press `F6` to select the field. To select more than one field, press `Tab` or `Shift`+`Tab`. When finished selecting fields, press `Enter`.
4. To move the selected field(s), you must press `F7` (Move), move the cursor to where the field(s) should be positioned, and then press `Enter`.

....

RENAMING VIEW FIELDS

If you want your view to display a different field name than that used in the database file structure, you can rename the field using the Edit field name option in the Fields menu. The new field name must still be a valid dBASE field name; that is, you can't use spaces or more than 10 characters.

Perform the following steps to rename the CUSTNUM field as NUMBER:

1. First remove the TITLE, ADDRESS, STATE, and ZIP fields from the view so that fewer fields are displaying.

2. To rename the CUSTNUM field, you must first position the cursor in the view skeleton. If the cursor isn't already positioned in the view skeleton, press (F3).

3. The cursor should be positioned in the view skeleton.
    PRESS: (Tab) *until the CUSTNUM field is highlighted*

4. To display the Fields menu:
    PRESS: (Alt)+F

5. Choose the Edit field name option.

6. TYPE: NUMBER
    PRESS: (Enter)
    The new field name should now be displaying in the view skeleton.

7. To view the data:
    PRESS: (F2)
    Note that the CUSTNUM field is now named NUMBER.

8. To display the Queries design screen:
    PRESS: (Shift)+(F2)

....

Quick Reference   1. Display the Queries design screen.
Renaming a   2. To rename a field, you must first press (F3) to position the cursor in
View Field   the view skeleton.
                         3. Highlight the field to be renamed.
                         4. Choose the Edit field name option from the Fields menu.
                         5. Type the new field name and press (Enter).

....

SAVING AND DESCRIBING VIEW QUERIES

Once you've decided how you want your view to look, you can save the view skeleton so you can use it at a later date without having to go through all the steps to create the view.

When saving, you can:

- Save the query and then remain in the Queries design screen. This is accomplished by choosing the Save this query option from the Layout menu.
- Save the query and then exit to the Control Center. This is accomplished by choosing the Save changes and exit option from the Exit menu.

In both cases, you must name the file with between one and eight characters; as mentioned earlier, dBASE automatically supplies the extension of QBE to all query files.

....

Quick Reference   1. Display the Queries design screen.
Saving Without   2. Choose the Save this query option from the Layout menu.
Exiting   3. Type in a name for the query file, and then press (Enter).

....

....

Quick Reference   1. Display the Queries design screen.
Saving and   2. Choose the Save changes and exit option from the Exit menu.
Exiting to the   3. Type in a name for the query file, and then press (Enter).
Control Center

....

Before saving a view, it's a good idea to enter a description for the view to help you remember what the purpose of the view is. This is especially important as you create additional views. To do this, you can choose the Edit description of query option from the Layout menu. After entering a description, you should name the query using one of the previously described procedures.

Quick Reference
Describing a
View Query

1. Display the Queries design screen.
2. Choose the Edit description of query option from the Layout menu.
3. Type in a description and then press (Enter). The description will be saved when you save the query file.

In the following steps you will enter a description for the current view and then save the current view as CUST1 using the Save this query option from the Layout menu:

1. The Queries design screen should be displaying on the screen. To enter a description for the current view, choose the Edit description of query option from the Layout menu.

2. Type the following description of the current view:
   TYPE: Listing of selective fields; the CUSTNUM field (named NUMBER) has been moved
   PRESS: (Enter)

3. The Queries design screen should again be displaying. To save the view, choose the Save this query option from the Layout menu.

4. dBASE is now prompting you for a name:
   TYPE: CUST1
   PRESS: (Enter)
   The current view has been saved and the Queries design screen is still displaying on the screen.

ORGANIZING VIEW RECORDS

dBASE provides several methods for organizing database records, or displaying them in a different order. You can organize database records with or without the use of an index (you learned how to create indexes in Session 2). *However, when you organize a database without the use of an index, the resulting view is read-only; that is, you can't edit any of the records when displaying the view data.* If you order your view data by a field that has an associated index file, your view won't be read-only. In addition, when using an index file, dBASE takes less time to put the database in order. Therefore, it is recommended to use existing indexes or to create indexes for the database file before organizing your view records. In the next few sections we lead you through organizing a database with and without the use of one or more indexes.

ORGANIZING WITHOUT AN INDEX

To organize, or sort, view records into a certain order, you must type a sort operator (Table 3.2) beneath the field you want to sort on. (*Note*: When organizing a view, the term *sort* doesn't imply that a copy of the database will be made.) For example, if you want the CUSTOMER database to be listed in ascending order by the CITY field, you would type ASC1 beneath the CITY field name in the file skeleton. If you want the secondary sort key to be the LASTNAME field, you would type ASC2 beneath the LASTNAME field (Figure 3.3).

Table 3.2	*Name*	*Example*	*Purpose*
Different Sort Types	Ascending ASCII	0...9, A...Z, a...z	The sort will be case sensitive.
	Descending ASCII	z...a, Z...A, 9...0	The sort will be case sensitive.
	Ascending Dictionary	0...9, Aa...Zz	The sort won't be case sensitive.
	Descending Dictionary	zZ...aA, 9...0	The sort won't be case sensitive.

After typing sort information beneath the appropriate field names, to display the data in sorted order, press (F2). To illustrate:

1. Make sure the CUSTOMER database is the active database and that you've chosen the <create> marker in the Queries panel.

2. Remove the TITLE, ADDRESS, STATE, and ZIP fields from the view.

3. Use (Tab) to position the cursor beneath the CITY field.

Figure 3.3

Organizing a database. In this example, the CITY field is the primary sort key, and the LAST-NAME field is the secondary sort key.

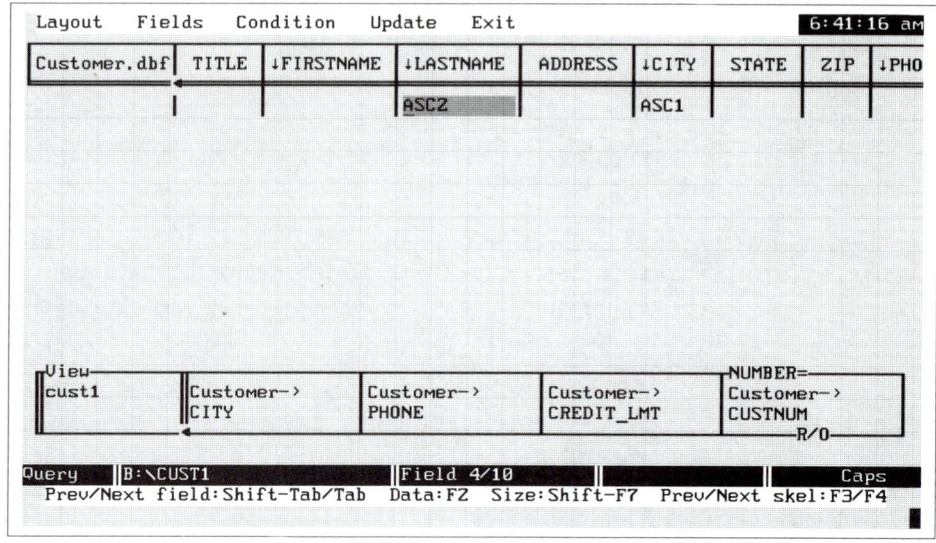

4. To specify that you want the database sorted into order by the CITY field:
   TYPE: ASC1

5. To display the view in sorted order:
   PRESS: [F2]
   Note that the "ReadOnly" indicator appears on the status line. As mentioned earlier, at this point you can't make changes to your database since you're sorting the database without the use of an index.

6. To display the Queries design screen:
   PRESS: [Shift]+[F2]

7. To sort on a secondary field, position the cursor in the LASTNAME field.

8. With the cursor in the LASTNAME field:
   TYPE: ASC2

9. To display the view in sorted order:
   PRESS: [F2]
   The screen should look like Figure 3.4. The data is displaying in order by the CITY field; the records for each city are in order by the LASTNAME field.

Figure 3.4

The CUSTOMER database is in order by the CITY field; the records for each city are in order by the LASTNAME field.

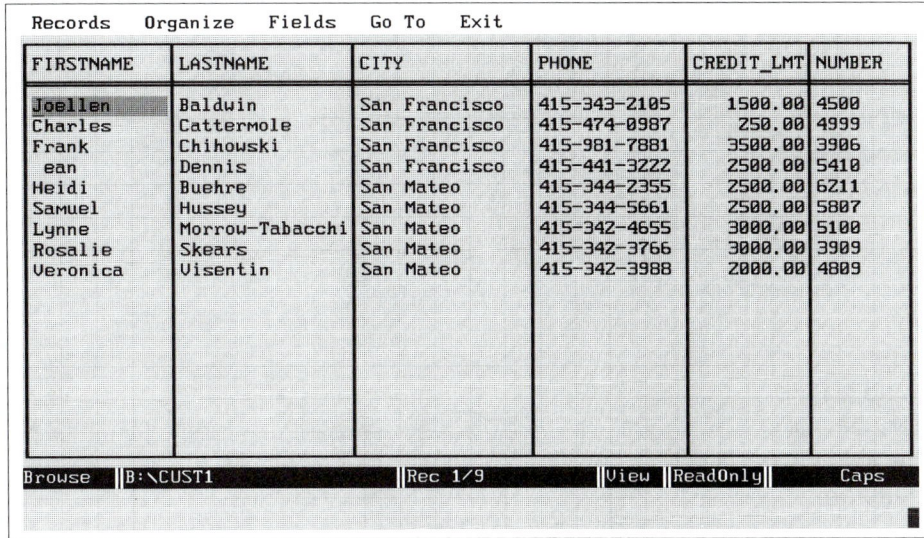

10. To display the Queries design screen:
    PRESS: (Shift)+(F2)

11. To display the Control Center, choose the Save changes and exit option from the Exit menu. The query file will be named CUST1 since you named the view CUST1 previously.

ABOUT ORGANIZING WITH AN INDEX

If you have already created indexes to be used with the active file (creating and using indexes were described in Session 2), you should set the Include indexes option in the Fields menu to YES. When this option is chosen, a triangle will appear next to every field in the file skeleton that has an associated index. (*Note*: If you are using an early version of dBASE IV, a # sign may display instead of the triangle.) If you created a **complex index**, an index that is based on more than one field, a triangle or # sign followed by the index expression will be listed at the right end of the file skeleton (Figure 3.5). A complex index looks like it's a field in the file skeleton; however, it isn't. For this reason, the complex index field is often referred to as a **pseudo-field**. Organizing on a field that already has an associated index is faster than sorting on one that doesn't.

Figure 3.5

Displaying indexes using the INVNTORY database. After indexes have been included, any complex indexes will be listed on the right end of the file skeleton.

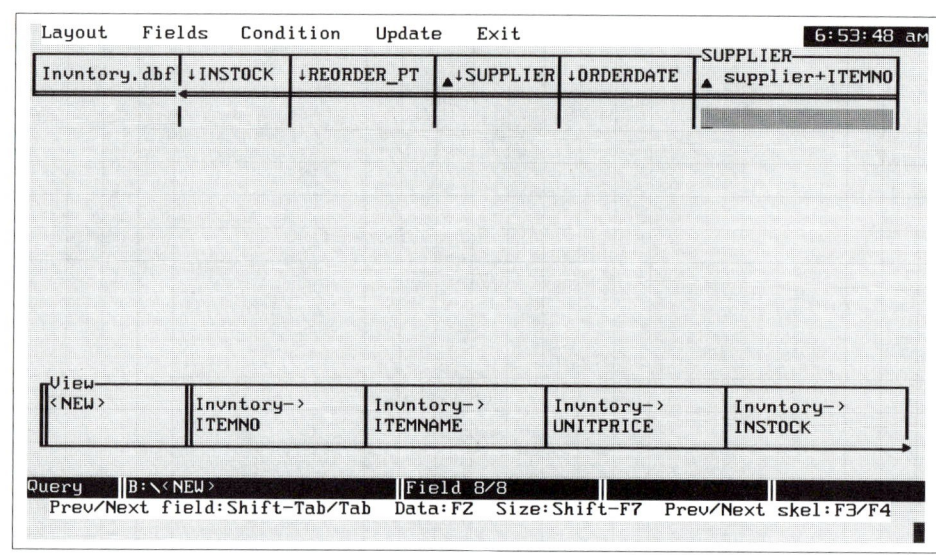

In the next few sections you will use the INVNTORY database that is stored on the Advantage Diskette to practice organizing the database using indexed fields. This database has an associated INVNTORY.MDX file which contains three index tags.

DETERMINING WHICH FIELDS HAVE AN ASSOCIATED INDEX

In the steps below you will work with the INVNTORY database that is stored on the Advantage Diskette to practice using the Queries design screen to organize database records. Before organizing on an indexed field, you must determine which fields have an associated index. To do this, perform the following steps:

1. The Control Center should be displaying on the screen. Highlight INVNTORY in the Data panel, press (Enter), and then choose the Use file option. The INVNTORY database is now the active database.

2. To display the Queries design screen, highlight the <create> marker in the Queries panel, and then press (Enter). The file and view skeletons for the INVNTORY database should be displaying on the screen.

3. To see what data is stored in the INVNTORY database:
    PRESS: (F2)
    The screen should now look like Figure 3.6.

Figure 3.6

INVNTORY
database
listing

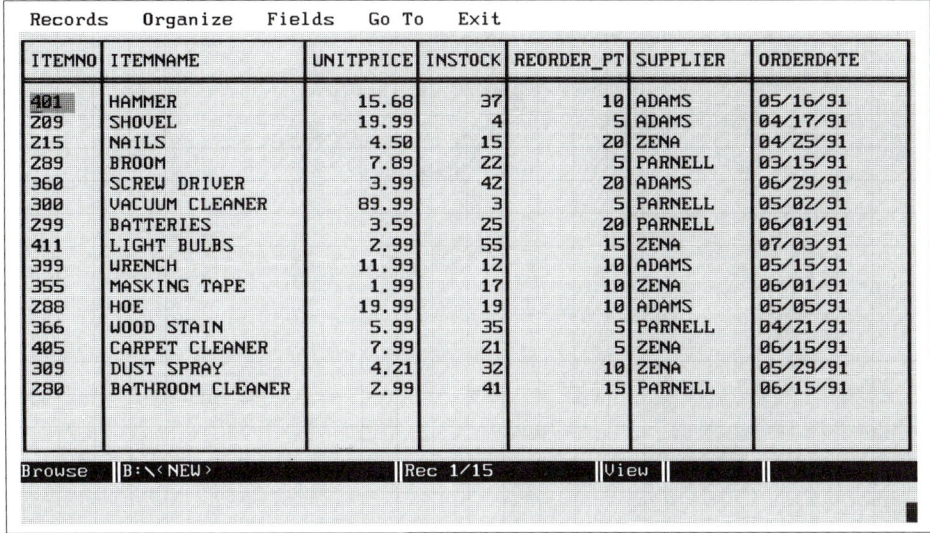

```
   Records    Organize    Fields    Go To    Exit

   ITEMNO  ITEMNAME            UNITPRICE INSTOCK REORDER_PT SUPPLIER  ORDERDATE

   401     HAMMER                15.68     37        10    ADAMS     05/16/91
   209     SHOVEL                19.99      4         5    ADAMS     04/17/91
   215     NAILS                  4.50     15        20    ZENA      04/25/91
   289     BROOM                  7.89     22         5    PARNELL   03/15/91
   360     SCREW DRIVER           3.99     42        20    ADAMS     06/29/91
   300     VACUUM CLEANER        89.99      3         5    PARNELL   05/02/91
   299     BATTERIES              3.59     25        20    PARNELL   06/01/91
   411     LIGHT BULBS            2.99     55        15    ZENA      07/03/91
   399     WRENCH                11.99     12        10    ADAMS     05/15/91
   355     MASKING TAPE           1.99     17        10    ZENA      06/01/91
   288     HOE                   19.99     19        10    ADAMS     05/05/91
   366     WOOD STAIN             5.99     35         5    PARNELL   04/21/91
   405     CARPET CLEANER         7.99     21         5    ZENA      06/15/91
   309     DUST SPRAY             4.21     32        10    ZENA      05/29/91
   280     BATHROOM CLEANER       2.99     41        15    PARNELL   06/15/91


   Browse   B:\<NEW>                        Rec 1/15         View
```

4. To display the Queries design screen:
   PRESS: [Shift]+[F2]

5. At this point, nothing on the screen shows what fields have associated indexes. To see what fields have an associated index, choose the Include indexes option from the Fields menu so that the status of this option is set to YES.

6. Note that the first two fields in the file skeleton have a triangle or a # sign next to them. If one of these symbols is displaying next to a field, the field has an associated index file.

7. To display the last field in the file skeleton:
   PRESS: [Tab] *until the right side is in view*
   The screen should look like Figure 3.5. The last field, a pseudo-field, isn't really a field; it is a complex index.

....

Quick Reference
Determining Which
Fields Have an
Associated Index

1. Display the Queries design screen.
2. Choose the Include indexes option from the Fields menu so the option is set to YES.
3. A triangle or # sign will appear next to every field in the file skeleton that has an associated index.

....

ORGANIZING ON A SINGLE-FIELD INDEX

The procedure to organize a view using a single-field index is very straightforward. Simply position the cursor beneath an indexed field and type in the appropriate sort operator (Table 3.2). In the steps below, you will organize the database by the ITEMNAME field (which does have an associated index).

1. Position the cursor beneath the ITEMNAME field in the file skeleton.

2. To sort in ascending order:
   TYPE: ASC1
   The screen should look like Figure 3.7.

Figure 3.7

This simple index will order the database by the ITEM-NAME field.

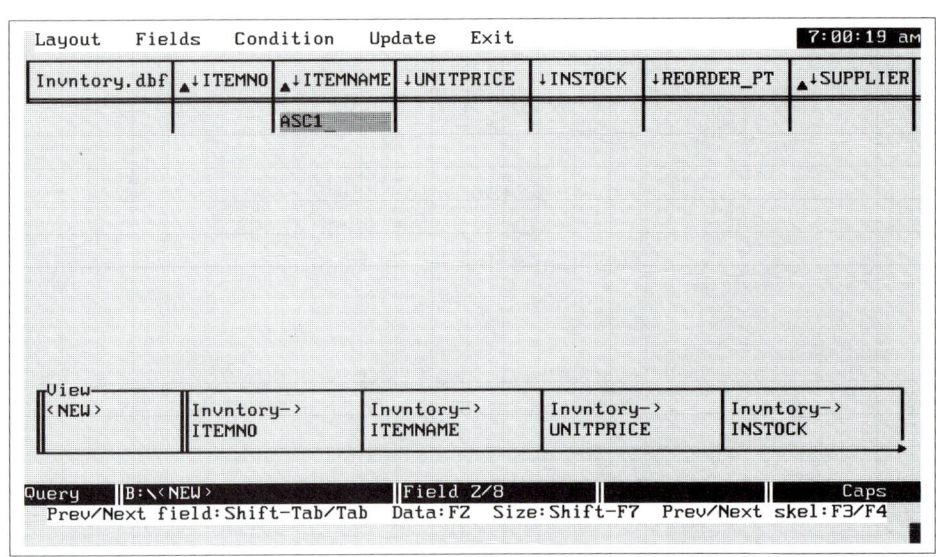

3. To view the data:
   PRESS: [F2]
   The database should be listed on the screen in order by the ITEMNAME field. Note that no ReadOnly indicator appears. Because your reorganization is based on an indexed field, you can edit the data at this point, if necessary.

4. To display the Queries design screen:
   PRESS: [Shift]+[F2]

5. On your own, display the data in ascending order based on the ITEMNO field. *Note*: You will first need to press (Delete) to delete the ASC1 text from the ITEMNAME field.

Quick Reference
Organizing on a Single-Field Index

1. Display the Queries design screen.
2. Position the cursor beneath a field that contains an index. An indexed field is marked by the # sign.
3. Type in a sort operator.
4. Press (F2) to view the data.

ORGANIZING ON A MULTIPLE-FIELD INDEX

The procedure to organize a view using a multiple-field index is identical to that for organizing on a single-field index except that the sort operator is typed in beneath the complex index, or pseudo-field. To illustrate, perform the following steps:

1. Delete any sort operators that may be displaying in the ITEMNO or ITEMNAME fields.

2. Press (Tab) until the cursor is displaying beneath the complex index on the right side of the file skeleton.

3. To sort in ascending order:
   TYPE: ASC1
   The screen should look like Figure 3.8.

4. To view the data:
   PRESS: (F2)
   The database should be listed on the screen in order by SUPPLIER and all the supplier records should be in order by the ITEMNO field. Note that no ReadOnly indicator appears. Again, because your sort is based on an indexed field, you can edit the data at this point, if necessary.

5. To display the Queries design screen:
   PRESS: (Shift)+(F2)

Figure 3.8

This complex index will order the database by the SUPPLIER and ITEMNO fields.

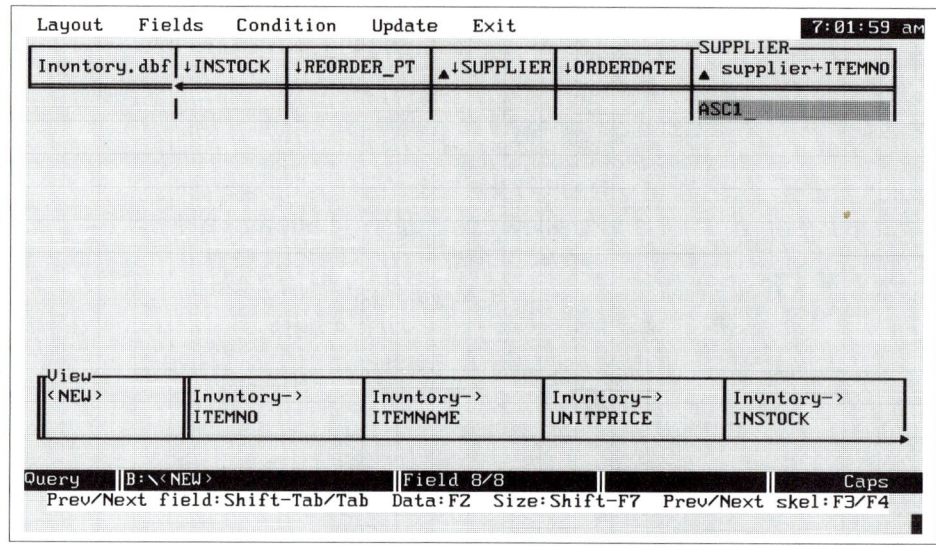

Quick Reference
Organizing on a Multiple-Field Index

1. Display the Queries design screen.
2. Position the cursor beneath a pseudo-field that contains a complex index (on the right side of the file skeleton).
3. Type in a sort operator.
4. Press (F2) to view the data.

ADDING A CALCULATED FIELD IN A VIEW

dBASE makes it possible to add up to 20 calculated fields in a view. A calculated field is added horizontally to the end of the view skeleton. For example, in the view of the INVNTORY database, it would be nice to include a field that calculates the value of inventory by multiplying UNITPRICE * INSTOCK. By including this calculated field in the view, you can determine the inventory value of each item. The field could be named something like INV_VALUE.

To include a calculated field in the view of the INVNTORY database, perform the following steps:

1. Make sure the INVNTORY database is the active database.

2. Display the Queries design screen by choosing the <create> marker in the Queries panel.

3. The INVNTORY database file skeleton should be displaying on the screen. To add a calculated field, choose the Create calculated field option from the Fields menu.

4. dBASE is now waiting for you to type in a valid dBASE expression telling it what fields to include in the calculation and what operation to perform.
   TYPE: INSTOCK*UNITPRICE
   PRESS: (Enter)

5. Now you need to name the calculated field. To do this, choose the Edit field name option from the Fields menu.

6. To name the field INV_VALUE:
   TYPE: INV_VALUE
   PRESS: (Enter)
   The screen should look like Figure 3.9. Note that the field name now appears above the calculated fields expression.

Figure 3.9

Defining a calculated field. This is what your screen looks like after you have specified what fields should be used in the calculation and have named the field.

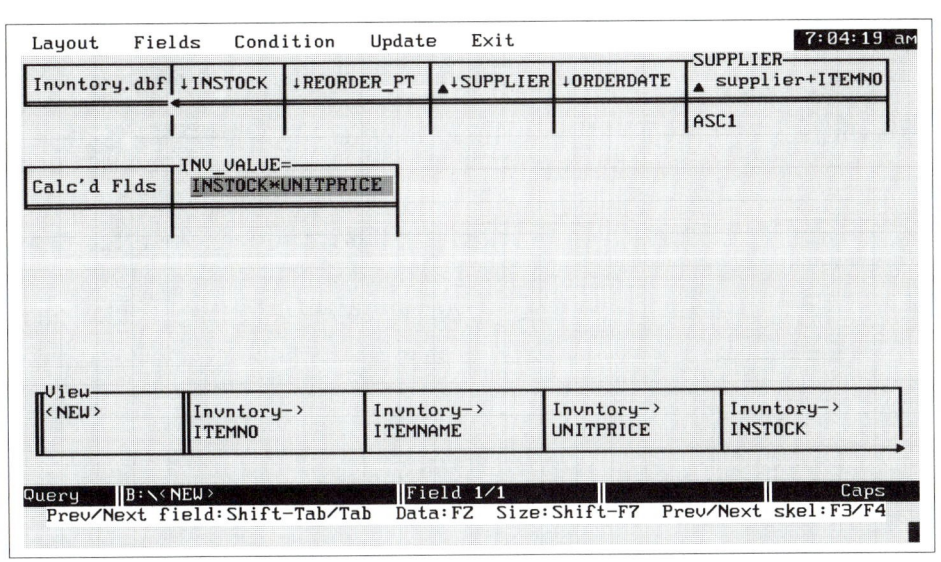

7. Now that you've named the calculated field, you must add the field to the view skeleton on the bottom of the screen. To do this, choose the Add field to view option in the Fields menu.

8. To see that the field was added to the view, press F3 until the cursor is in the view skeleton on the bottom of the screen. Then press Tab until you can see the calculated field.

9. To display the view:
PRESS: F2
You may need to press Tab to view the calculated field (Figure 3.10). (*Note*: You can't change the width of a calculated field except when you create a report; you learn how to create reports in Session 4.)

Figure 3.10

Viewing the calculated field. INV_VALUE multiplies the UNITPRICE field by the INSTOCK field.

Records	Organize	Fields	Go To	Exit	

UNITPRICE	INSTOCK	REORDER_PT	SUPPLIER	ORDERDATE	INV_VALUE
19.99	4	5	ADAMS	04/17/91	79.96
19.99	19	10	ADAMS	05/05/91	379.81
3.99	42	20	ADAMS	06/29/91	167.58
11.99	12	10	ADAMS	05/15/91	143.88
15.68	37	10	ADAMS	05/16/91	580.16
2.99	41	15	PARNELL	06/15/91	122.59
7.89	22	5	PARNELL	03/15/91	173.58
3.59	25	20	PARNELL	06/01/91	89.75
89.99	3	5	PARNELL	05/02/91	269.97
5.99	35	5	PARNELL	04/21/91	209.65
4.50	15	20	ZENA	04/25/91	67.50
4.21	32	10	ZENA	05/29/91	134.72
1.99	17	10	ZENA	06/01/91	33.83
7.99	21	5	ZENA	06/15/91	167.79
2.99	55	15	ZENA	07/03/91	164.45

Browse	B:\<NEW>		Rec 2/15	View		Caps

A calculated field is read-only; in other words, you can't edit the contents of a calculated field. However, if you make a change to one of the fields upon which the calculated field is dependent, the value in the calculated field will automatically update to display the correct answer.

10. To display the Queries design screen:
PRESS: Shift+F2

11. To save the view query as INV1, choose the Save changes and exit option from the Exit menu.

12. dBASE is now prompting you for a name:
TYPE: INV1
PRESS: Enter
The Control Center should be displaying on the screen.

1. To add a calculated field, choose the Create calculated field option from the Fields menu.
2. Type in the valid dBASE expression upon which calculations will be based.
3. To name the calculated field, choose the Edit field name option from the Fields menu.
4. To add the field to the view skeleton, choose the Add field to view option in the Fields menu.
5. To display the view:
    PRESS: F2

SEARCHING A DATABASE

So far you've learned how to view all the records stored in a database. What if you only want to display a few records? For example, when working with a CUSTOMER database, what if you only want to list on the screen the records of customers who live in San Francisco? Using the Queries design screen, you can be selective about the records that are listed on the screen (or printed). In other words, you can search for data that meet your criteria. In the next few sections we lead you through using the CUSTOMER database, stored on the Advantage Diskette, to be selective about the records that are displayed on the screen. You will create and save three separate view queries. You will create the following three view files:

1. VIEW1 enables you to view those records that have credit limit amounts (CREDIT_LMT) greater than 2000.

2. VIEW2 enables you to view a listing of all customers who live in San Mateo.

3. VIEW3 enables you to view those customers who live in an Mateo (CITY) and who have a credit limit greater than 2000.

In the next few steps, you will create a view named VIEW1 that will enable you to view those records that have credit limit amounts (CREDIT_LMT) greater than 2000. Perform the following steps:

1. The Control Center should be displaying on the screen. Make the CUSTOMER database the active database.

2. Highlight the <create> marker in the Queries panel and press (Enter).
   The Queries design screen should now be displaying.

3. Position the cursor beneath the CREDIT_LMT field.
   TYPE: >2000
   The screen should look like Figure 3.11.

Figure 3.11

Search conditions. The condition of >2000 was typed in below the CREDIT_LMT field. The result of this condition is shown in Figure 3.12.

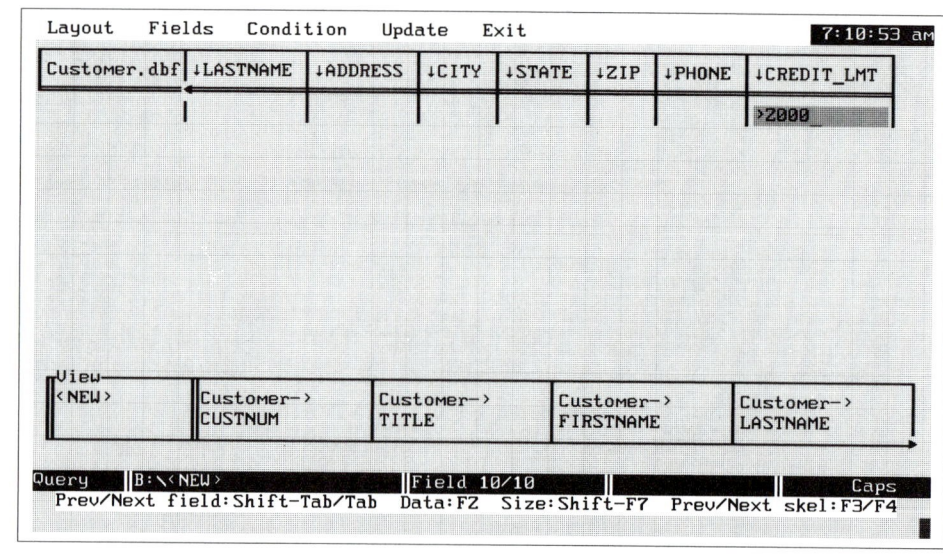

4. To view the data:
   PRESS: (F2)
   The screen should look like Figure 3.12. Only those customers who have a credit limit greater than $2000 are listed on the screen.

5. To display the Queries design screen:
   PRESS: (Shift)+(F2)

Quick Reference
Viewing
Selected
Records

1. Display the Queries design screen by highlighting the <create> marker in the Queries panel.
2. Position the cursor beneath the field name that your search is based on.
3. Type in your search condition.
4. Press (F2) to view the data.

Figure 3.12

Because of the CREDIT_LMT field condition shown in Figure 3.11, only those records in the CUSTOMER database that contain a credit limit amount greater than 2000 will be listed on the screen.

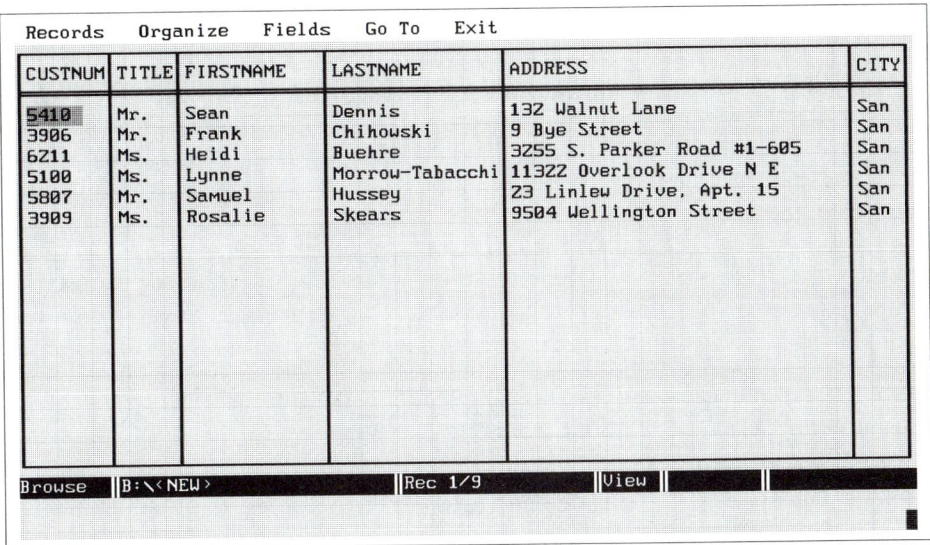

To save the view skeleton so you can use it at a later date without having to go through all the steps to create the view, perform the following steps:

1. To activate the Exit menu:
    PRESS: Alt+E

2. Choose the Save changes and exit option.

3. dBASE is now prompting you to type in a filename for the view skeleton.
    TYPE: VIEW1
    PRESS: Enter
    The Control Center should be displaying on the screen.

To create a view named VIEW2 that will enable you to view a listing of all customers who live in San Mateo, perform the following steps:

1. The Control Center should be displaying on the screen. Make sure the CUSTOMER database is the active database.

2. Highlight the <create> marker in the Queries panel and press Enter. The Queries design screen should now be displaying.

3. Position the cursor beneath the CITY field.
    TYPE: "San Mateo"

(*Note*: The character string *San Mateo* must be typed exactly as you keyed it into the database initially; for example, if you capitalized the *S* of *San* and the *M* of *Mateo*, you must do so here. Or if you typed *San Mateo* all uppercase, you must do so here. In addition, the character string must be surrounded by quotes.)

4. To view the data:
   PRESS: [F2]
   After pressing [Tab] a few times, you can see that the records that have a CITY field that is equal to San Mateo are now listed on the screen.

5. To display the Queries design screen:
   PRESS: [Shift]+[F2]

To save the view skeleton so you can use it at a later date without having to go through all the steps to create the view, perform the following steps:

1. To activate the Exit menu:
   PRESS: [Alt]+E

2. Choose the Save changes and exit option.

3. dBASE is now prompting you to type in a filename for the view skeleton.
   TYPE: VIEW2
   PRESS: [Enter]
   The Control Center should be displaying on the screen.

To create a view named VIEW3 that will enable you to view those customers who live in San Mateo (CITY) and who have a credit limit that is greater than $2000, perform the following steps:

1. The Control Center should be displaying on the screen. Make sure the CUSTOMER database is the active database.

2. Highlight the <create> marker in the Queries panel and press [Enter]. The Queries design screen should now be displaying.

3. Position the cursor beneath the CITY field.
   TYPE: "San Mateo"

4. Position the cursor beneath the CREDIT_LMT field.
   TYPE: >2000
   The screen should look like Figure 3.13.

Figure 3.13

Including more than one condition below a field heading in the same row represents an AND condition. (If the conditions are on different rows, an OR condition exists.)

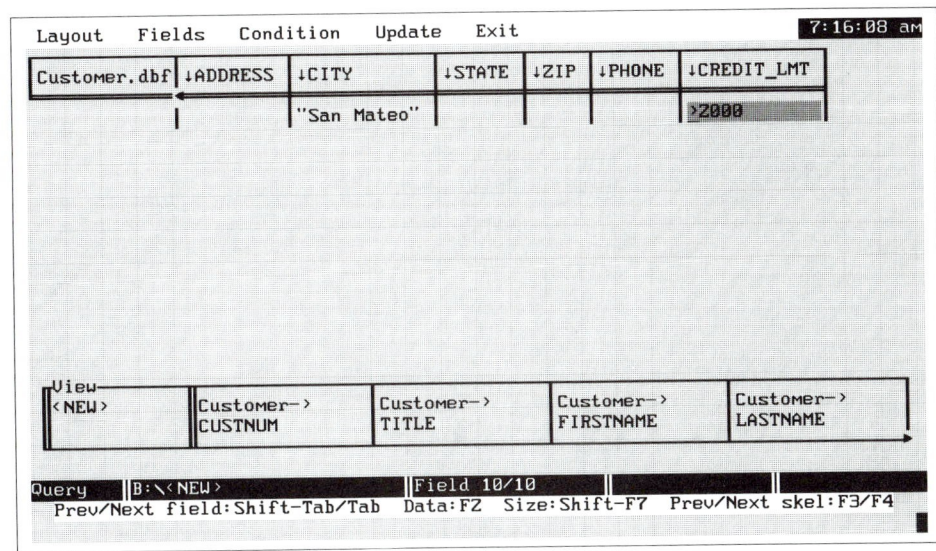

5. To view the data:
PRESS: [F2]
Two records should be displaying that meet your search criterion.

6. To view the Queries design screen:
PRESS: [Shift]+[F2]

To save the view skeleton so you can use it at a later date without having to go through all the steps to create the view, perform the following steps:

1. To activate the Exit menu:
PRESS: [Alt]+E

2. Choose the Save changes and exit option.

3. dBASE is now prompting you to type in a filename for the view skeleton.
TYPE: VIEW3
PRESS: [Enter]
The Control Center should be displaying on the screen.

dBASE makes it possible to view almost any information you're interested in. For example, Figure 3.14 pictures the conditions necessary to view those records that have a credit limit amount that is greater than 200 and less than 3000. Figure 3.15 pictures the conditions necessary to view those records that have a credit limit that is either less than 300 or greater than

2000 (to specify an OR condition, you must put the conditions on separate lines).

Figure 3.14

Searching for those customers who have a credit limit amount greater than 200 and less than 3000.

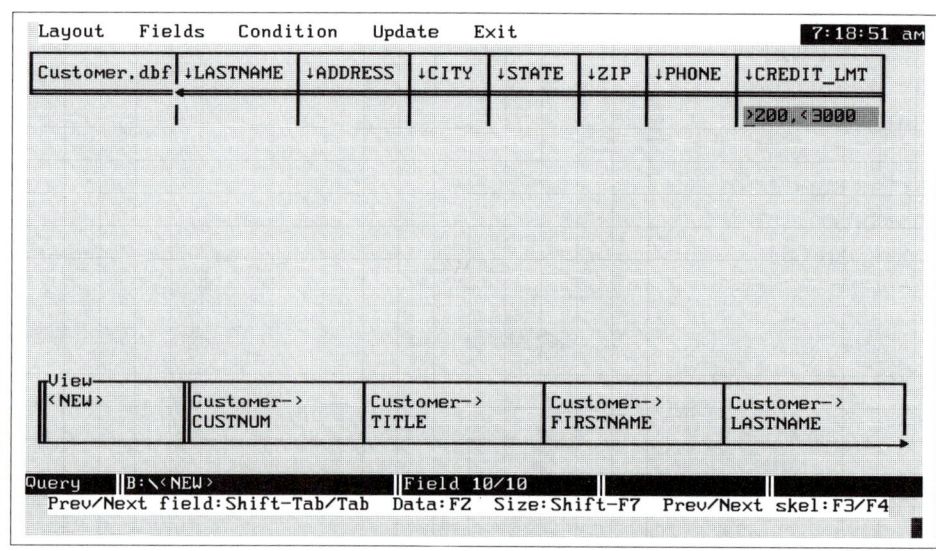

Figure 3.15

Searching for those customers who have a credit limit amount less than 300 or greater than 2000.

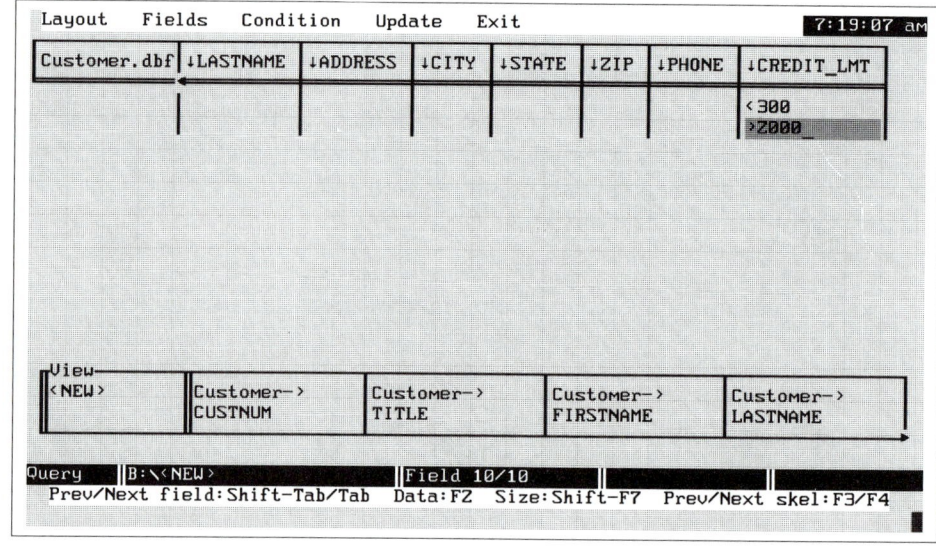

SUMMARY

In this session, you learned how use the Queries design screen to create view queries, which provide the user with a view, or partial picture, of the data stored in a database file. You learned how to choose specific fields to be viewed and how to filter out irrelevant records from your screen display. The basic steps to create and use view queries typically include:

- Use, or open, a database file
- Decide what fields to display in the view
- Decide what records to display in the view
- Display the data using F2
- Name and save the view query

The records in a view can be organized with an index or without. Organizing a database on an indexed field, however, typically saves processing time. To organize the records in a view, you must type a sort operator beneath the field or pseudo-field, that you want the view to be ordered by.

COMMAND SUMMARY

The table on the next few pages provides a list of the commands and procedures covered in this session.

Table 3.3 Command Summary	Removing a Field from a View	1. Display the Queries design screen. 2. Highlight the field you want to remove. 3. Choose the Remove field from view option from the Fields menu, or press F5.
	Adding a Field to a View	1. Display the Queries design screen. 2. Position the cursor in the field to be added. 3. Choose the Add field to view option from the Fields menu, or press F5.

Table 3.3 Command Summary (continued)	Removing a Field from a View	1. Display the Queries design screen. 2. Highlight the field you want to remove. 3. Choose the Remove field from view option from the Fields menu, or press F5.
	Adding a Field to a View	1. Display the Queries design screen. 2. Position the cursor in the field to be added. 3. Choose the Add field to view option from the Fields menu, or press F5.
	Removing and Adding All Fields in a View	1. Display the Queries design screen. 2. Position the cursor beneath the filename in the file skeleton, and press F5 once or twice to remove or add all the fields in the view.
	Displaying and Printing Data in a View	While viewing the Queries design screen: 1. Press F2 to display your data. At this point, if necessary, you can edit the data viewed. You can print the displayed data by pressing Shift+F9 and then choosing the Begin printing option. 2. To return to the Queries design screen, press Shift+F2. While viewing the Control Center: Highlight the view file in the Queries panel (view files have the extension of QBE) and press F2.
	Renaming a View Field	1. Display the Queries design screen. 2. To rename a field, you must first press F3 to position the cursor in the view skeleton. 3. Highlight the field to be renamed. 4. Choose the Edit field name option from the Fields menu. 5. Type the new field name and press Enter.

Table 3.3 Command Summary (continued)	Moving Fields	1. Display the Queries design screen. 2. Press F3 to position the cursor in the view skeleton. 3. Highlight the field you want to move, and then press F6 to select the field. To select more than one field, press Tab or Shift+Tab. When finished selecting fields, press Enter. 4. To move the selected field(s), you must press F7 (Move), move the cursor to where the field(s) should be positioned, and then press Enter.
	Saving Without Exiting	1. Display the Queries design screen. 2. Choose the Save this query option from the Layout menu. 3. Type in a name for the query file, and then press Enter.
	Saving and Exiting to the Control Center	1. Display the Queries design screen. 2. Choose the Save changes and exit option from the Exit menu. 3. Type in a name for the query file, and then press Enter.
	Describing a View Query	1. Display the Queries design screen. 2. Choose the Edit description of query option from the Layout menu. 3. Type in a description and then press Enter. The description will be saved when you save the query file.
	Determining Which Fields Have an Associated Index	1. Display the Queries design screen. 2. Choose the Include indexes option from the Fields menu so the option is set to YES. 3. A triangle or # sign will appear next to every field in the file skeleton that has an associated index.

Table 3.3	Organizing on a Single-Field Index	1. Display the Queries design screen. 2. Position the cursor beneath a field that contains an index. An indexed field is marked by a triangle or # sign. 3. Type in a sort operator. 4. Press F2 to view the data.
Command Summary (concluded)	Organizing on a Multiple-Field Index	1. Display the Queries design screen. 2. Position the cursor beneath a pseudo-field that contains a complex index (on the right side of the file skeleton). 3. Type in a sort operator. 4. Press F2 to view the data.
	Adding a Calculated Field	1. To add a calculated field, choose the Create calculated field option from the Fields menu. 2. Type in the valid dBASE expression upon which calculations will be based. 3. To name the calculated field, choose the Edit field name option from the Fields menu. 4. To add the field to the view skeleton, choose the Add field to view option in the Fields menu. 5. To display the view: PRESS: F2
	Viewing Selective Records	1. Display the Queries design screen by highlighting the <create> marker in the Queries panel. 2. Position the cursor beneath the field name that your search is based on. 3. Type in your search condition. 4. Press F2 to view the data.

KEY TERMS

complex index   An index based on more than one field.

file skeleton   In dBASE IV, when the user is creating view queries, the file skeleton displays; it is a graphic representation of the active database file, showing the names of all the fields in the database.

pseudo-field   In dBASE IV, a field in the file skeleton consisting of a multiple-field, or complex, index.

view query   In dBASE IV, a view query provides a partial picture of the data stored in a database file.

view skeleton   Format for the current view query.

EXERCISES

SHORT ANSWER

1. What is the Queries design screen used for?
2. How do you move the cursor from field to field in the Queries design screen?
3. What is a pseudo-field?
4. What key is used to remove fields from and add fields to a view?
5. What is the procedure for adding a calculated field to a view?
6. Why is it advantageous to organize a database on an indexed field?
7. Once you've created a view of your database, how do you display the data? What would you need to do before you can display the view data at a later time?
8. What are the basic steps involved with creating and using view queries?
9. A company database contains a field named DEPT. What would you have to do to display on the screen the records relating to department B?
10. What is a complex index?

HANDS-ON

1. To practice using the Queries design screen, perform the following
    steps using the EMP-DATA database:
    a. List all the records.
    b. Use the Queries design screen to:
        -   List the following fields on the screen: TITLE, LASTNAME,
            CITY, and HIREDATE
        -   List the following fields on the screen for those employees who
            live in San Mateo: TITLE, LASTNAME, CITY, and
            HIREDATE
        -   List the same fields as in the previous step, except search for
            those employees who live in San Francisco.

2. To practice using the Queries design screen, perform the following
    steps using the INV-DATA database:
    a. List all the records.
    b. List the ITEMNO, INSTOCK, and REORDER_PT fields.
    c. List those records that have an INSTOCK value that is less than 10.
    d. List the ITEMNO and ITEMNAME fields for those records that
        have an INSTOCK value that is less than 15.
    e. Move the SUPPLIER field so it is the first field listed in the view.
    f. Include a calculated field named STATUS that subtracts the
        REORDER_PT field from the INSTOCK field. Add the STATUS
        field to the view.
    g. Save the current view as STATUS.

3. Using the EXP-DATA database, perform the following steps:
    a. List all the records and fields in the EXPENSES database.
    b. List all the records but only the ITEM_DESC and EXP_AMOUNT
        fields.
    c. List all the records and fields in the EXPENSES database that have
        the word PHONE in the CATEGORY field.
    d. Print a list of only the OFFICE expenses.

4. To practice creating a calculated field, create a calculated field in the
    INVOICE database named INVAMT that multiplies the UNITPRICE
    field by the QUANTITY field. Add the calculated field to the view.
    Print a listing of all the records in the INVOICE database, however
    include only the INVNUM, ITEMNAME, QUANTITY, UNITPRICE,
    and INVAMT fields in the listing.

CREATING FORMS, REPORTS, AND LABELS

In the last three sessions you learned how to use a number of database management systems (DBMS) software commands to help you create, manage, and retrieve information from a database. In this session you will learn how to "dress up" your screen display and the information you retrieve from a database. This session will help you understand why DBMS software is so popular in the business environment.

PREVIEW

When you have completed this session, you will be able to:

Create forms for data entry and editing.
·
Create quick and custom reports.
·
Create mailing labels.

Why Is This Session Important?
Creating Forms
      Quick Form Layout
      Removing a Field
      Adding and Labeling a Field
      Inserting Labels and Spaces
      Removing and Adding Lines
      Adding a Box
      Saving the Form
      Viewing and Modifying an Existing
        Form
Creating Reports
      Creating a Quick Report
      The Reports Design Screen
      Changing the Header and Detail
        Bands
      Saving a Report Format
      Viewing and Printing a Report
      Modifying a Report
Creating Labels
      Creating the Label Form
      Saving the Label Form
      Viewing and Printing Labels
Summary
      Command Summary
Key Terms
Exercises
      Short Answer
      Hands-On

WHY IS THIS SESSION IMPORTANT?

In this session you learn how to display the data stored in a database in different ways to suit your business and personal needs. You learn how to customize the data entry screen using the Forms design screen, and how to create custom report listings using the Reports design screen.

Before proceeding, make sure the following are true:

1. You have loaded dBASE IV and are displaying the Control Center.

2. Your Advantage Diskette is inserted in the drive. You will save your work onto the diskette and retrieve the files that have been created for you. (*Note*: The Advantage Diskette can be made by copying all the files off the instructor's Master Advantage Diskette onto a formatted diskette.)

3. You have changed the current drive to the one that contains your Advantage Diskette. Remember that dBASE assumes the hard disk is the current drive until you change the drive. Refer to the section on Changing the Current Drive in Session1 if necessary.

CREATING FORMS

When you edit data in the Browse or Edit screens, your data is displayed in a predictable format. In Edit mode, one record at a time is visible on the screen at a time; in Browse mode, the records in your database are displayed in a table format, with each row of information representing a different record in the database. It is impossible to change the standard format of the Browse screen; however, by creating a form you can change the way your data appears in the Edit screen. A **form** is a screen through which you can look at and modify the data stored in a database or view. Forms are used to customize the screen display and to make data entry easier. In addition, forms are often used to hide parts of a database from view. For example, when using an employee database, you might want to keep the salary information hidden from the view of some database users.

Forms are created using the Forms design screen, which creates a file with the extension of SCR. When you use a form, it automatically references, or points to, the underlying data in a database file. The four basic elements of a form are:

- Fields that relate to a database or view
- Calculated fields that aren't in a database or view
- Descriptive text
- Boxes and lines

Figure 4.1 shows a form as it is being created in the Forms design screen and Figure 4.2 shows the completed form as the user would see it on the screen during data entry or while performing editing tasks.

Figure 4.1

Using the Forms design screen to create a form for the CUSTOMER database

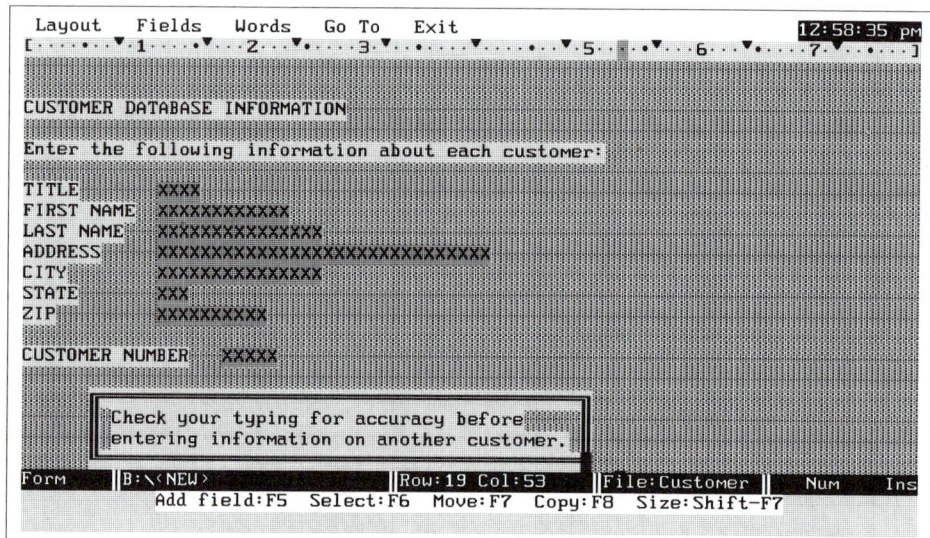

QUICK FORM LAYOUT

The **quick form layout** displays each of the field names in your database down the left side of your screen (Figure 4.3). The quick form layout is rarely used in its original form, because it looks like the Edit mode screen; rather, it is modified by removing or moving fields, including descriptive text, and/or by including a box around the form.

Figure 4.2

A completed form. This form was created to be used with the CUSTOMER database.

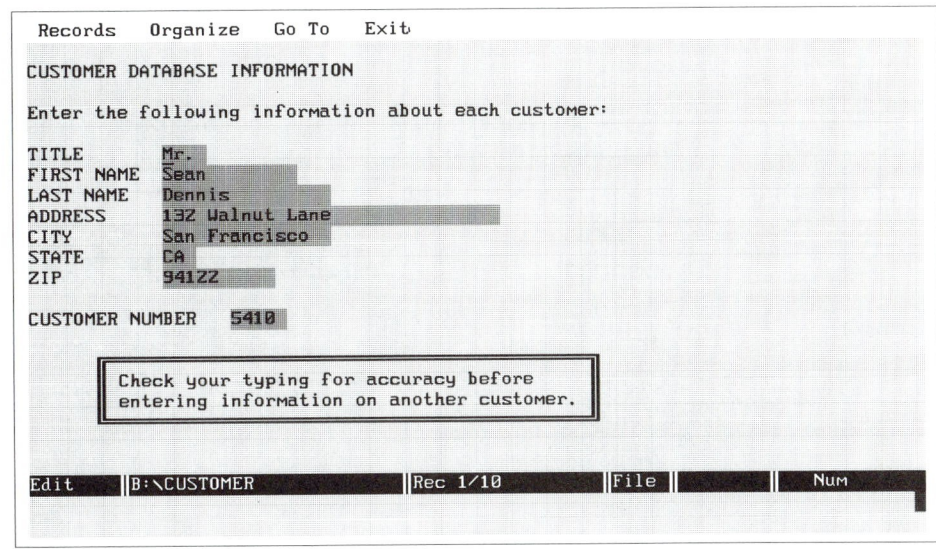

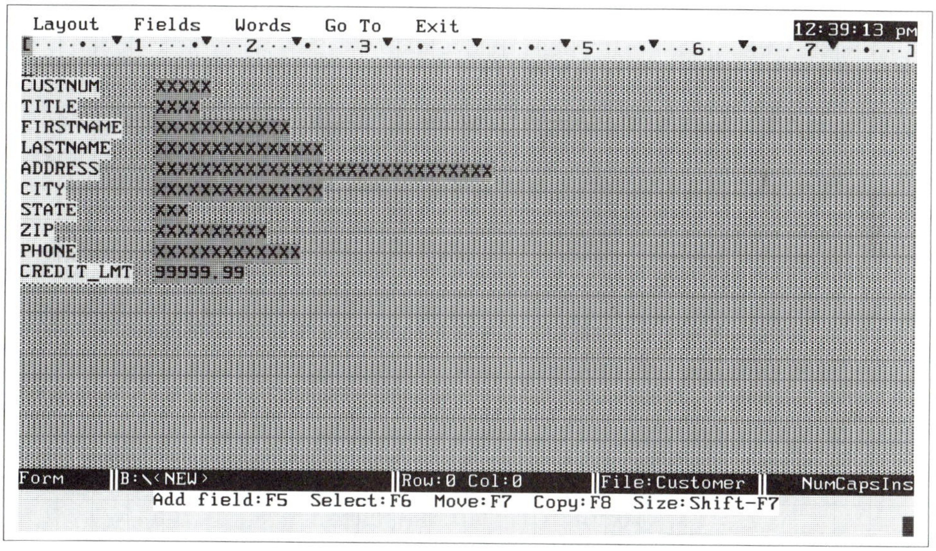

In this section you will create a quick form for the CUSTOMER database. In later sections you will modify this form to practice using additional commands.

1. Make sure the CUSTOMER database, stored on the Advantage Diskette, is the active database.

Figure 4.3

Quick form layout

2. The Control Center should be displaying on the screen. To enter the Forms design screen, highlight the <create> marker in the Forms panel and press (Enter).

3. The Layout menu should be displaying. Choose the Quick layout option from the Layout menu. Your screen should look like Figure 4.3.

What do you see? In the quick layout, each field name in the database is positioned at the left margin. To the right of each field name is the field **template**. This template shows the width and type of the field data. An X represents character data, whereas a 9 represents numeric data. Date fields are represented by MM/DD/YY, and logical fields are represented by Ys. *The first line of this screen, line 0, is blank so that the Edit menu can display. Make sure to always leave line 0 blank.*

....

Quick Reference   1. Make sure a database is active.
Creating a   2. From the Control Center, to enter the Forms design screen,
Quick Layout   highlight the <create> marker in the Forms panel and press (Enter).
                        3. The Layout menu should be displaying. Choose the Quick layout
                           option from the Layout menu.

....

REMOVING A FIELD

A commonly used procedure for creating a form is to first create the quick layout of the form and to then delete the fields that you don't want displayed in the form. In this section you will remove the CUSTNUM, PHONE, and CREDIT_LMT fields.

To remove the text associated with a field (for example, CUSTNUM), position the cursor beneath the first character of text and press (Delete) until the text is deleted. To remove a field's template, choose the Remove field option from the Fields menu, and then the field you want to remove. (*Note*: You can delete a field's template also by positioning the cursor in the field template and pressing (Delete)). In the following steps, you will use the Fields menu to remove the fields.

Perform the following steps:

1. To remove the CUSTNUM field, choose the Remove field option of the Fields menu. A list of field names should be displaying on the screen.

2. Choose the CUSTNUM field. The template for the CUSTNUM field has now disappeared.

3. To delete the text CUSTNUM, position the cursor beneath the *C* of CUSTNUM and press ⌈Delete⌋ until CUSTNUM disappears.

4. Using the same procedure as described in steps 1–3 above, remove the PHONE and CREDIT_LMT fields. The screen should look like Figure 4.4.

Figure 4.4

The CUSTNUM, PHONE, and CREDIT_LMT field templates and corresponding text have been removed from the Forms design screen.

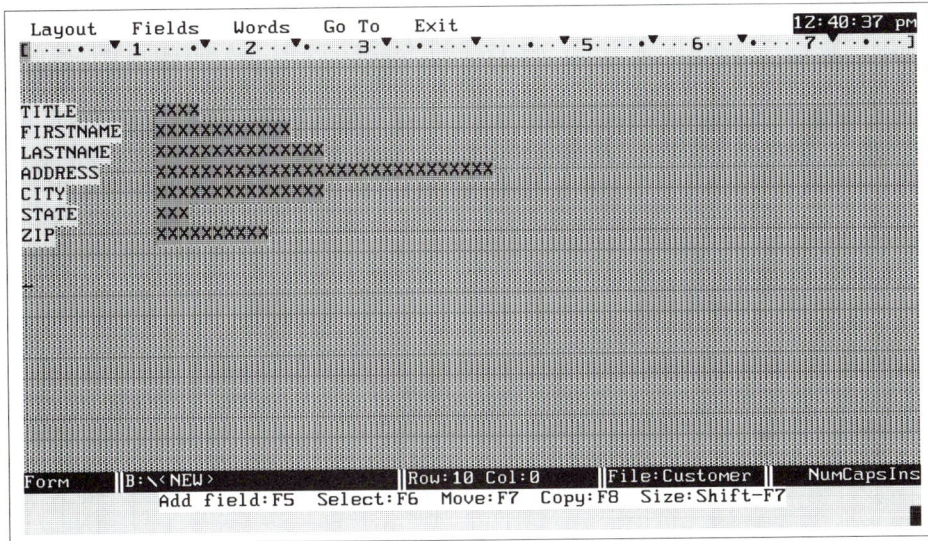

```
   Layout   Fields   Words   Go To   Exit                    12:40:37 PM
[ · · · · ▼ · 1 · · · · ▼ · · · 2 · · · · ▼ · · · 3 · ▼ · · · · · ▼ · · 5 · · · ▼ · · · 6 · · · ▼ · · · · · 7 · ▼ · · · · ]

   TITLE     XXXX
   FIRSTNAME XXXXXXXXXXX
   LASTNAME  XXXXXXXXXXXXXX
   ADDRESS   XXXXXXXXXXXXXXXXXXXXXXXXXXXX
   CITY      XXXXXXXXXXXXXX
   STATE     XXX
   ZIP       XXXXXXXXX




 Form    ║B:\<NEW>                ║Row:10 Col:0   ║File:Customer ║  NumCapsIns
          Add field:F5   Select:F6   Move:F7   Copy:F8   Size:Shift-F7
```

Quick Reference
Removing a Field

1. While displaying the Forms design screen, choose the Remove field option from the Fields menu.
2. Choose the field you want to remove from the field list.
3. Delete the field name using ⌈Delete⌋.

ADDING AND LABELING A FIELD

If you have a database that contains many fields, but only want to include a few fields in a form, it may be faster to add the fields to the form (as opposed to generating the quick form layout, and then removing the fields you don't want to include). To add a field to a form, choose the Add field option from the Fields menu.

In this step, you will add the template for the CUSTNUM field to the form, and label the template CUSTOMER NUMBER. Perform the following steps:

1. Before adding a field, you must position the cursor where you want the descriptive text to be positioned. Position the cursor two lines below the ZIP field, against the left margin.

2. Instead of labeling the field CUSTNUM, type the following descriptive text:
   TYPE: CUSTOMER NUMBER

3. To move the cursor to where the field template should be positioned:
   PRESS: → three times

4. To include the template for the CUSTNUM field, choose the Add field option from the Fields menu. A list of field names should be listed on the screen.

5. Choose the CUSTNUM field by highlighting it and pressing Enter.

6. dBASE is now displaying the characteristics of the CUSTNUM field. To place the field on the Forms design screen:
   PRESS: Ctrl + End
   The template for the CUSTNUM field should now be displaying on the screen.

Quick Reference
Adding and Labelling a Field

1. While displaying the Forms design screen, position the cursor where you want the field text to be positioned, and then type the text.
2. Position the cursor where the field template should be positioned, and then choose the Add field option of the Fields menu.
3. Choose the name of the field to be added.

INSERTING LABELS AND SPACES

Once the appropriate fields are positioned on the Forms design screen, you may want to insert additional spaces or descriptive text. On the Forms design screen, dBASE operates in Insert mode. Therefore, any characters you type will be inserted at the cursor position. In addition, if you press

(Enter), any characters to the right of the cursor will be moved down to the next line.

In the following steps you will insert a few blank lines at the top of the form and additional text to describe the form. When you finish, the screen will look like Figure 4.5.

Figure 4.5

Adding descriptive text to the Forms design screen

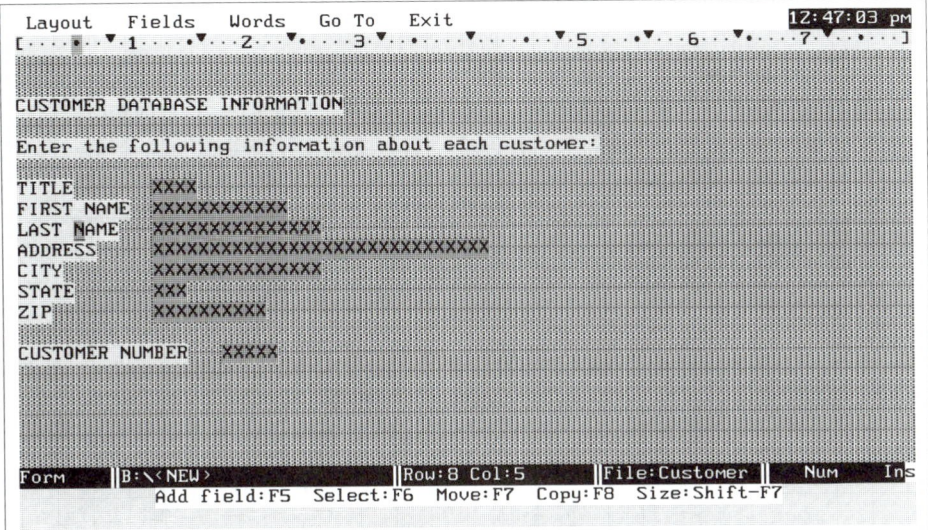

```
 Layout   Fields   Words   Go To   Exit                    12:47:03 pm
[····■··▼·1····▼··2···▼··3·▼····▼····▼·5···▼·6··▼··▼·7·▼····]

CUSTOMER DATABASE INFORMATION

Enter the following information about each customer:

TITLE        XXXX
FIRST NAME   XXXXXXXXXXX
LAST NAME    XXXXXXXXXXXXX
ADDRESS      XXXXXXXXXXXXXXXXXXXXXXXXXXXX
CITY         XXXXXXXXXXXXX
STATE        XXX
ZIP          XXXXXXXXXX

CUSTOMER NUMBER   XXXXX




Form     B:\<NEW>              Row:8 Col:5    File:Customer   Num    Ins
              Add field:F5  Select:F6  Move:F7  Copy:F8  Size:Shift-F7
```

1. To insert a few blank lines above the TITLE field and to then insert a heading for the Forms design screen, position the cursor beneath the first *T* of TITLE, and then press (Enter) a few times.

2. Position the cursor two lines above the TITLE field.

3. To enter a heading and some additional text:
   TYPE: CUSTOMER DATABASE INFORMATION
   PRESS: (Enter) *twice*
   TYPE: Enter the following information about each customer:

4. Position the cursor beneath the *N* in the FIRSTNAME field.

5. To insert a space between FIRST and NAME:
   PRESS: Space Bar

6. Using the same procedure as in steps 4–5, insert a space between LAST and NAME. The screen should look like Figure 4.5.

REMOVING AND ADDING LINES

To delete a line that is either blank or contains data, you must position the cursor on the line you want to remove (or delete) and then choose the Remove line option from the Words menu. The line will be removed and anything below the line will be moved up one line. The Add line option of the Words menu is used to insert a blank line in a form; as described in the last section, you can also insert a line by pressing [Enter].

Quick Reference
*Removing and
Adding Lines*

1. While displaying the Forms design screen, to remove a line, position the cursor on the line you want to remove, and then choose the Remove line option of the Words menu.
2. To add, or insert, a line, position the cursor where the line should be inserted, and then choose the Add line option of the Words menu.

ADDING A BOX

Boxes are often used in forms to make certain text stand out so that it can be spotted easily. To add a box, you must choose the Box option of the Layout menu, and then either the single- or double-underline option. Next, you must position the cursor where the upper-left corner of the box should be positioned and press [Enter]. To complete the box, use the cursor-movement keys to frame the text, and then press [Enter].

Perform the following steps to insert text on the bottom of the form, and then frame the text with a box:

1. Position the cursor three lines below the CUSTOMER NUMBER field information.

2. Type the following text:
   PRESS: [Tab] *to move the cursor away from the left margin*
   TYPE: Check your typing for accuracy before
   PRESS: [Enter]
   PRESS: [Tab]
   TYPE: entering information on another customer.

3. To surround the text with a box, choose the Box option of the Layout menu.

4. Choose the Double line option.

5. dBASE now wants you to position the cursor in the location of the upper-left corner of the box. Using the cursor-movement keys, position the cursor one line above the text and a few spaces to the left.

6. To mark the upper-left corner of the box:
PRESS: Enter

7. Press ↓ a few times and then → until the text is framed with a box.

8. Once the text is framed with a box:
PRESS: Enter
The screen should look like Figure 4.1.

Quick Reference
Adding a
Box

1. While displaying the Forms design screen, choose the Box option of the Layout menu.
2. Choose the single- or double-underline option.
3. Position the cursor where the upper-left corner of the box should be positioned and press Enter.
4. To complete the box, use the cursor-movement keys to frame the text, and then press Enter.

SAVING THE FORM

Once you've created a form, you should save it so you can use it later. To save a form and then remain in the Forms design screen, choose the Save this form option of the Layout menu. To save a form and then exit to the Control Center, choose the Save changes and exit option of the Exit menu. In both cases, you will need to give the form a name with between one and eight characters.

To save the current form as FORM1 and then exit to the Control Center:

1. Choose the Save changes and exit option of the Exit menu.

2. dBASE is now waiting for you to type in a form name:
TYPE: FORM1
PRESS: Enter
The form has been saved and the Control Center should be displaying on the screen.

Quick Reference
*Saving the
Form*

- To save a form and then remain in the Forms design screen, choose the Save this form option of the Layout menu. **Type a name** for the form and then press [Enter].
- To save a form and then exit to the Control Center, **choose the** Save changes and exit option of the Exit menu. **Type a name for** the form and then press [Enter].

VIEWING AND MODIFYING AN EXISTING FORM

To view the form, highlight the name of the form in the Forms panel of the Control Center and then press [F2] (Data). The form will display on the screen. (Pressing [F2] again will display the database data in Browse mode.) *Once you've finished entering data using the form, press* [Ctrl]+[End] *to return to the Control Center.*

1. To view the form:
    PRESS: [F2]

2. To display the Control Center:
    PRESS: [Ctrl]+[End]

To modify an existing form, highlight the name of the form in the Forms panel and then press [Enter]. Choose the Modify layout option. The Forms design screen will display on the screen. When you are finished making changes, make sure to save your work.

Quick Reference
*Viewing an
Existing Form*

Highlight the name of the form in the Forms panel, and then press [F2]. To return to the Control Center, press [Ctrl]+[End].

Quick Reference
*Modifying an
Existing Form*

Highlight the name of the form in the Forms panel, and then press [Enter]. Choose the Modify layout option. To return to the Control Center, press [Ctrl]+[End].

CREATING REPORTS

Reports enable you to display the data in your database in a format more stylized than the data display obtained using Browse mode or the Queries design screen. dBASE enables you to create two types of reports: quick reports and custom reports. The **quick report** option provides a simple means for you to generate a report of your database file or current view. It automatically inserts the current date and page number in the upper-left corner of the screen and automatically totals numeric fields. The headings for each of the columns in the report are the field names you defined in your database. You cannot make any changes to a quick report. Figure 4.6 pictures a quick report of the INVNTORY database.

Figure 4.6

Quick report. This INVNTORY report listing was generated using Shift+F9.

```
Page No.   1
01/14/93

ITEMNO  ITEMNAME          UNITPRICE  INSTOCK  REORDER_PT  SUPPLIER  ORDERDATE

401     HAMMER               15.68      37         10      ADAMS     05/16/91
209     SHOVEL               19.99       4          5      ADAMS     04/17/91
215     NAILS                 4.50      15         20      ZENA      04/25/91
289     BROOM                 7.89      22          5      PARNELL   03/15/91
360     SCREW DRIVER          3.99      42         20      ADAMS     06/29/91
300     VACUUM CLEANER       89.99       3          5      PARNELL   05/02/91
299     BATTERIES             3.59      25         20      PARNELL   06/01/91
411     LIGHT BULBS           2.99      55         15      ZENA      07/03/91
399     WRENCH               11.99      12         10      ADAMS     05/15/91
355     MASKING TAPE          1.99      17         10      ZENA      06/01/91
288     HOE                  19.99      19         10      ADAMS     05/05/91
366     WOOD STAIN            5.99      35          5      PARNELL   04/21/91
405     CARPET CLEANER        7.99      21          5      ZENA      06/15/91
309     DUST SPRAY            4.21      32         10      ZENA      05/29/91
280     BATHROOM CLEANER      2.99      41         15      PARNELL   06/15/91
                            203.77     380        165

         Cancel viewing: ESC,  Continue viewing: SPACEBAR
```

The **custom report** option provides greater reporting flexibility, enabling you to design all the features that you want to include in the report. With this command you can choose the fields to be included in the report and change the descriptive text that appears on the top of each column. In addition, you can add graphic elements, such as a line or a box, and add calculated fields that don't exist in your database file or view. You can also include page headers (text that appears on the top of each page) and page footers (text that appears on the bottom of each page) in your report. Once you have created a custom report, you can save it onto your disk so that you can use its specifications again. Figure 4.7 pictures a custom report of the INVNTORY database.

CREATING A QUICK REPORT

To create a quick report, highlight the name of the database in the Data panel and then press [Shift]+[F9]. Or, if you want to create a quick report of a view you saved using the Queries design screen, highlight the name of the view in the Queries panel and then press [Shift]+[F9]. In this section, you will create a quick report of the data stored in the INVNTORY database. Perform the following steps:

1. From the Control Center, highlight INVNTORY in the Data panel.

2. To format the database or view as a quick report, as indicated on the bottom of the screen:
    PRESS: [Shift]+[F9]

3. To view the report on the screen, choose the View report on screen option. The screen should look like Figure 4.6.

4. After viewing the quick report, press the Space Bar until the Control Center displays.

....

Quick Reference   1. From the Control Center, highlight the name of a database in the
Creating a   Data panel or the name of a view in the Queries panel.
Quick Report   2. PRESS: [Shift]+[F9]
                      3. To print the report, choose the Begin printing option. To view the
                          report on screen, choose the View report on screen option.

....

THE REPORTS DESIGN SCREEN

In this section you will create a custom report of the data stored in the INVNTORY database. When you finish, the report will look like Figure 4.7.

Perform the following steps:

1. Make sure the INVNTORY database is the active database.

2. Highlight the <create> marker in the Reports panel, and then press [Enter].

Figure 4.7

Custom report.
This report of the
INVNTORY data-
base was created
after choosing the
<create> marker
of the Reports
panel.

```
Page No.   1
01/14/93

ITEM     ITEM                UNIT      ITEMS     REORDER                ORDER
NUMBER   DESCRIPTION         PRICE     IN STOCK  POINT       SUPPLIER   DATE

401      HAMMER              15.68     37        10          ADAMS      05/16/91
209      SHOVEL              19.99      4         5          ADAMS      04/17/91
215      NAILS                4.50     15        20          ZENA       04/25/91
289      BROOM                7.89     22         5          PARNELL    03/15/91
360      SCREW DRIVER         3.99     42        20          ADAMS      06/29/91
300      VACUUM CLEANER      89.99      3         5          PARNELL    05/02/91
299      BATTERIES            3.59     25        20          PARNELL    06/01/91
411      LIGHT BULBS          2.99     55        15          ZENA       07/03/91
399      WRENCH              11.99     12        10          ADAMS      05/15/91
355      MASKING TAPE         1.99     17        10          ZENA       06/01/91
288      HOE                 19.99     19        10          ADAMS      05/05/91
366      WOOD STAIN           5.99     35         5          PARNELL    04/21/91
405      CARPET CLEANER       7.99     21         5          ZENA       06/15/91
309      DUST SPRAY           4.21     32        10          ZENA       05/29/91
280      BATHROOM CLEANER     2.99     41        15          PARNELL    06/15/91
                            203.77    380       165

_              Cancel viewing: ESC,  Continue viewing: SPACEBAR          ▌
```

The cursor should be highlighting the Quick layouts option. If this option is chosen, dBASE will include all fields in the active database in the report.

3. Choose the Quick layouts option.

    A few additional options should now be displaying. The Column layout option will display each of the fields in the active database side-by-side in a column format. Choosing the Form layout option will display each of the fields vertically down the left side of the screen; if you use this option, you aren't confined to a columnar format. Rather, fields can be positioned anywhere on the screen or printed page. The Mailmerge option enables you to position fields in order to generate form letters.

4. Choose the Column layout option. The display is initially confusing. Figure 4.8 helps to describe what you are looking at on the screen.

The Reports design screen is composed of a number of **bands** that are horizontal bars describing different sections of the report. These sections correspond to different locations on the printed report page. When you first enter the Reports design screen, dBASE makes certain assumptions, such as including all fields in a report. To customize a report to your needs, you can change these assumptions using the procedures described in this session.

Figure 4.8

Choosing the Column layout. (a) When you create a report, this screen appears after you choose the Column layout option. (b) This labeled report shows where each band is positioned on an actual printed report.

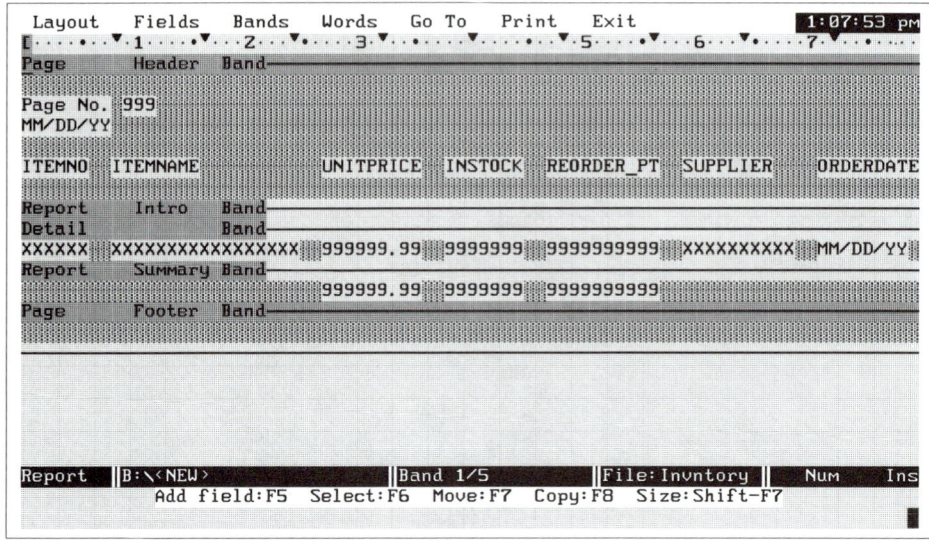

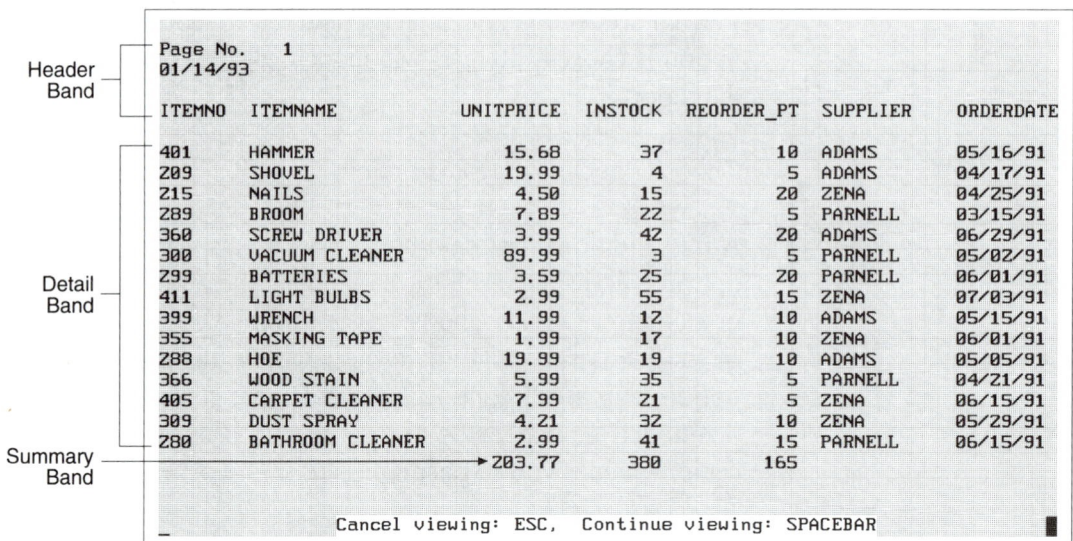

Initially, the following bands are included in the Reports design screen:

- *Report Intro Band.* The Report Introduction Band is used to enter a main title and descriptive text about the report; this information prints on the first page of the report.
- *Page Header Band.* The Header Band prints on the top of each page and includes the current page number and date, and the column headings for the report (if you chose the Column layout option). The column headings correspond to the field names as defined in the database structure.

- *Detail Band.* The Detail Band describes how the data in the body of the report will appear when printed. As described earlier, character fields are symbolized with a series of Xs, numeric fields with 9s, logical fields with Ys, and date fields with MM/DD/YY.
- *Summary Band.* The Summary Band includes the totals of the numeric fields in the report.
- *Page Footer Band.* The Page Footer will print on the bottom of every page. In a footer, you may want to include the current page number or date (if you have deleted it from the header), or descriptive text in the footer.

Note: When a band is open, the information in the band will print. When closed, it won't print. To open a band, position the cursor on the band and press (Enter). To close an open band, perform the same procedure.

CHANGING THE HEADER AND DETAIL BANDS

dBASE automatically includes the current page number and date in the Header Band of your report, along with the field names for every field in your database. To remove the page number and/or current date from the Header Band, position the cursor at the beginning of what should be deleted, and press (Delete) until the information is deleted.

To change the text for a particular column heading so that it is more descriptive, position the cursor on or near the text to be changed and insert or delete the appropriate text. If you don't want the detail information to display for a particular column, position the cursor in the appropriate field template in the Detail Band and then press (Delete) to delete the template. You should then delete the corresponding column heading.

In this section you will change some of the column heading text that currently appears in the Page Header Band.

1. Perform the following steps to insert a blank line in the Header Band:
   a. Position the cursor beneath the *I* of ITEMNO in the page header band.
   b. To insert a blank line:
      PRESS: (Enter)

2. To change the ITEMNO heading to ITEM NUMBER, with each word on a separate line:
   a. Position the cursor one line above the I of ITEMNO.
   b. TYPE: ITEM

    c. Delete the characters ITEMNO on the next line.
    d. TYPE: `NUMBER`

3. To change the ITEMNAME heading to ITEM DESCRIPTION, with each word on a separate line:
    a. Position the cursor one line above the *I* of ITEMNAME.
    b. TYPE: `ITEM`
    c. Delete the characters ITEMNAME on the next line.
    d. TYPE: `DESCRIPTION`

4. Change the rest of the headings so they look like those in Figure 4.7.

5. To view the report on the screen, choose the View report on screen option of the Print menu.

6. Press the Space Bar to redisplay the Reports design screen.

Quick Reference
Changing the
Header Band

1. To remove the page number and/or current date from the Header Band, use `Delete` to delete the information.
2. To change the text for a particular column heading, position the cursor on or near the text to be changed and insert or delete text.

Quick Reference
Changing the
Detail Band

If you don't want the detail information to display for a particular column, position the cursor in the appropriate field template in the Detail Band and press `Delete` to delete the template. Then delete the corresponding column heading.

SAVING A REPORT FORMAT

Once you've created a report and are pleased with how it looks, you can save the report specifications in a file using the Save changes and exit option of the Exit menu. If you don't want to exit the Reports design screen but want to save your work, choose the Save this report option of the Layout menu.

To save the report as REPORT1 and then exit to the Control Center:

1. Choose the Save changes and exit option of the Exit menu.

2. dBASE is now waiting for you to type a name.
   TYPE: REPORT1
   PRESS: [Enter]
   The report specifications are now saved on the disk and the Control Center should be displaying.

VIEWING AND PRINTING A REPORT

As described earlier, from the Reports design screen you can view a report on screen by choosing the View report on screen option of the Print menu; or you can print the report by choosing the Begin printing option of the Print menu.

If you've already saved the report and are viewing the Control Center, you can view or print a report by highlighting the name of the report in the Reports panel and pressing [Enter]. Then choose the Print report option or the Display data option.

MODIFYING A REPORT

To modify a report, highlight the report filename in the Reports panel of the Control Center and then press [Enter]. Choose the Modify layout option. After making changes to the report, save the report again.

Quick Reference
Modifying
a Report

1. Highlight the report filename in the Reports panel of the Control Center and then press (Enter).
2. Choose the Modify layout option.

CREATING LABELS

In this section you will create mailing labels for the data stored in the CUST1 database (stored on the Advantage Diskette). Figure 4.9 pictures the Labels design screen after you've defined what fields from your database should be included in the label. During a merge, the data from the database is inserted into the appropriate field locations in the label form; a different label is printed for each record in the database.

Figure 4.9

Using the Labels design screen to create mailing labels for the CUST1 database. Xs mark where the CUST1 field data will display after printing the labels.

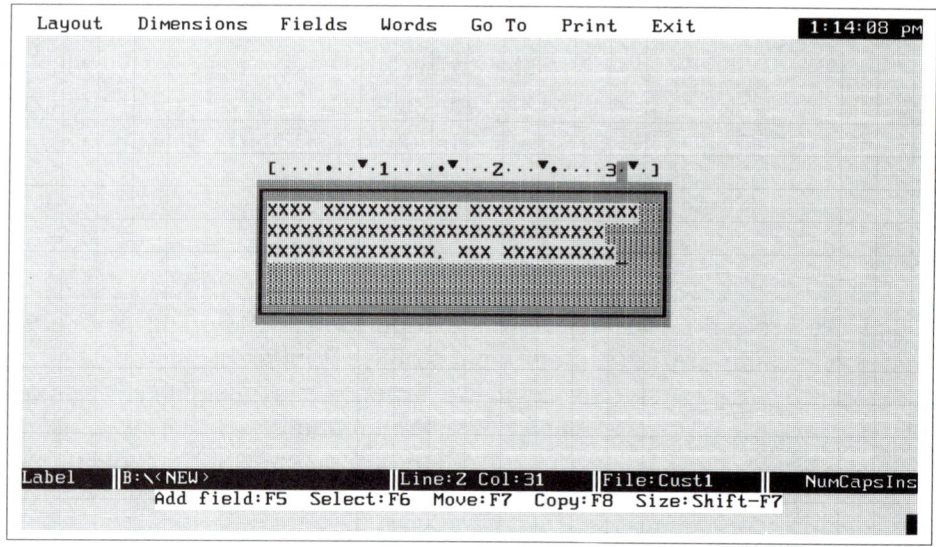

CREATING THE LABEL FORM

In this section you will include the following fields in a label form: TITLE, FIRSTNAME, LASTNAME, ADDRESS, CITY, STATE, and ZIP.

Perform the following steps to create a label form for the CUST1 database:

1. The Control Center should be displaying. Make sure the CUST1 database is the active database.

2. Highlight the <create> marker in the Labels panel and press [Enter]. The labels design screen should be displaying on the screen.

3. The cursor is positioned in the upper-left corner of the Labels screen. To include the TITLE field at the current cursor location:
   PRESS: [F5]

4. A list of field names should be displaying on the screen. Highlight the TITLE field and press [Enter].

5. To place the field in the Labels design screen:
   PRESS: [Ctrl]+[End]

6. Press the Space Bar once to include a space before the FIRSTNAME field.

7. To include the FIRSTNAME field at the current cursor location:
   PRESS: [F5]

8. A list of field names should be displaying on the screen. Highlight the FIRSTNAME field and press [Enter].

9. To place the field in the Labels design screen:
   PRESS: [Ctrl]+[End]

10. Press the Space Bar once to include a space before the LASTNAME field.

11. On your own, insert the LASTNAME, ADDRESS, CITY, STATE, and ZIP fields in the appropriate locations on the Labels design screen. When you finish, the Labels design screen should look like Figure 4.9.

SAVING THE LABEL FORM

Once you've created a label file and are pleased with how it looks, you can save it using the Save changes and exit option of the Exit menu. If you don't want to exit the Labels design screen but want to save your work, choose the Save this label design option of the Layout menu.

To save the label form as LABEL1 and then exit to the Control Center:

1. Choose the Save changes and exit option of the Exit menu.

2. dBASE is now waiting for you to type a name.
   TYPE: LABEL1
   PRESS: (Enter)
   The label form is now saved on the disk and the Control Center should
   be displaying.

Quick Reference   1. To save the label form and return to the Control Center, choose the
Saving a   Save changes and exit option of the Exit menu.
Label Form   2. If you don't want to exit the Labels design screen but want to save
                         your work, choose the Save this label design option of the Layout
                         menu.

VIEWING AND PRINTING LABELS

To view labels from the Control Center, highlight a label file in the Labels
panel and press (Enter). Choose the Print label option, and then the View
labels on screen option. To print the labels, choose the Begin printing
option in place of the View labels on screen option. To view or print the
labels from the Labels design screen, use the Print menu.

From the Control Center, perform the following steps to view the labels on
screen:

1. Highlight LABEL1 in the Labels panel and press (Enter).

2. Choose the Print label option, and then the View labels on screen
   option. The screen should look like Figure 4.10. Note that the labels
   are displaying down the left side of the page. Shortly you will learn
   how to display labels in more than one column on the page.

3. PRESS: Space Bar *to display the next screenful of labels*
   The appropriate names and addresses from the CUST1 database have
   been inserted in the LABEL1 label form.
   PRESS: Space Bar *to display the Control Center*

Figure 4.10

Viewing a single.
column of labels

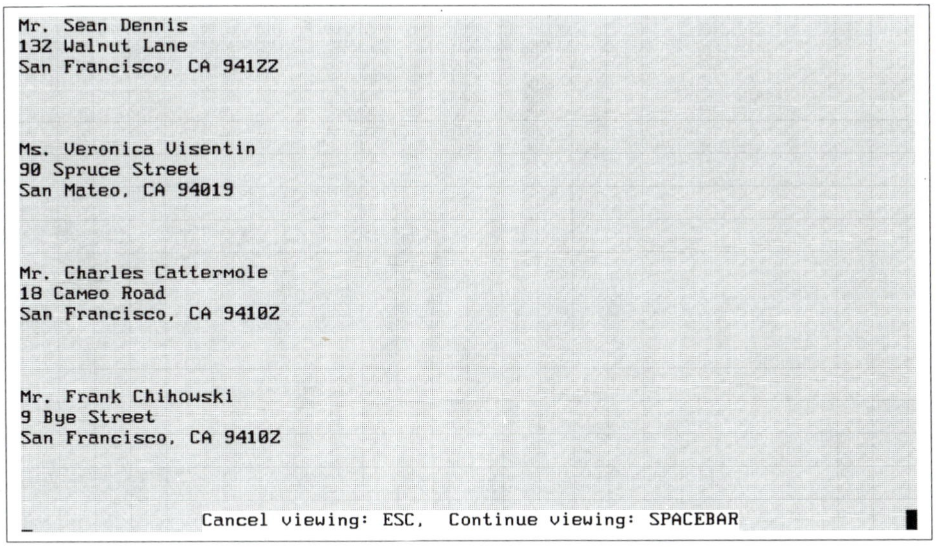

```
Mr. Sean Dennis
132 Walnut Lane
San Francisco, CA 94122



Ms. Veronica Visentin
90 Spruce Street
San Mateo, CA 94019



Mr. Charles Cattermole
18 Cameo Road
San Francisco, CA 94102



Mr. Frank Chihowski
9 Bye Street
San Francisco, CA 94102




             Cancel viewing: ESC,  Continue viewing: SPACEBAR
```

4. The Control Center should be displaying on the screen. To modify the label file so the labels are printed in two columns rather than one, highlight LABEL1 in the Labels panel and press (Enter).

5. Choose the Modify layout option.

6. Display the Dimensions menu (Figure 4.11). Using the options in this menu you can change the default assumptions dBASE makes about the labels you print.

7. Choose the Columns of labels option.

8. To display 2 columns of labels:
   TYPE: 2

9. To save the label form, choose the Save changes and exit option of the Exit menu.

10. The Control Center should again be displaying on the screen. View the labels on the screen (Figure 4.12).

Figure 4.11

The Dimensions
menu

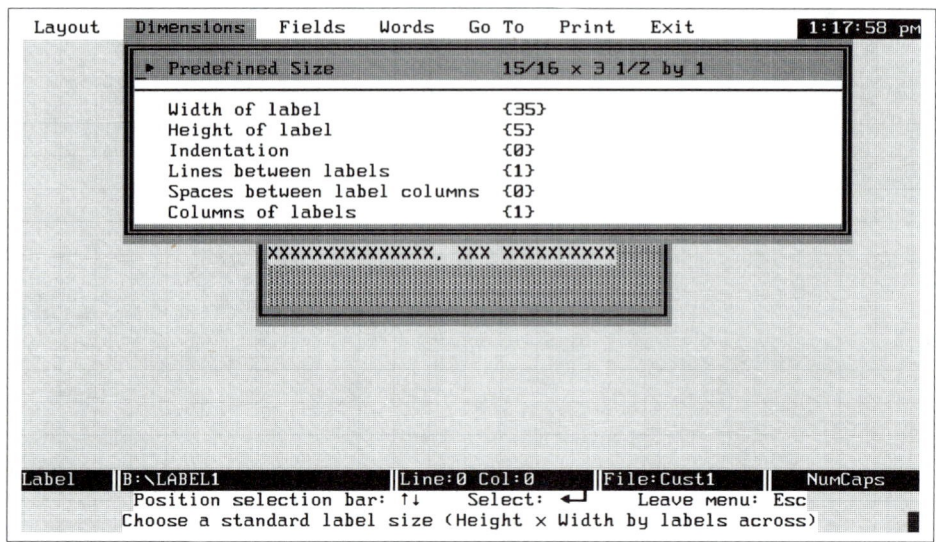

Figure 4.12

Viewing a double
column of labels.
Unless you choose
the Columns of
labels option of the
Dimensions menu,
dBASE will print
a single column of
labels.

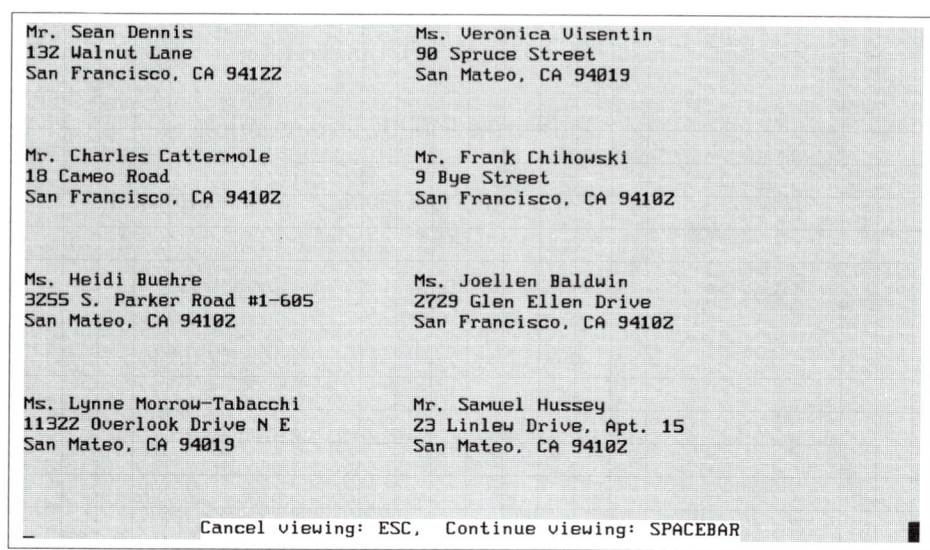

....

Quick Reference   1. Highlight the label name in the Labels panel and press (Enter).
Viewing   2. Choose the Print label option, and then the View labels on screen
Labels   option.

....

Quick Reference
*Modifying a
Label File*
1. Highlight the label name in the Labels panel and press (Enter).
2. Choose the Modify layout option.
3. After making changes to the label form, save the label using the Layout menu or the Exit menu.

SUMMARY

In this session you learned how to create forms, reports, and mailing labels. Each of these activities involves specifying the fields that should be included.

Forms are used to customize the screen display and to make data entry easier. Using the Forms design screen, you determine what fields to include in the form, as well as any descriptive text and boxes and/or lines.

dBASE enables you to use the Reports design screen to create two types of reports: quick reports and custom reports. The quick report option provides a simple means for you to generate a report of your database file or current view. It automatically inserts the current date and page number in the upper-left corner of the screen and automatically totals numeric fields. The custom report option provides greater flexibility because it enables you to choose the fields to be included in the report and to change the descriptive text that appears at the top of each column.

Using the Labels design screen, you can create mailing labels by choosing the fields to be included in the label form. When you print the mailing labels, the data from your database is inserted into the appropriate field locations in the label form; a different label is printed for each record in the database.

COMMAND SUMMARY

The table on the following pages provides a list of the commands and procedures covered in this session.

Table 4.1 Command Summary	Creating a Quick Layout	1. Make sure a database is active. 2. From the Control Center, highlight the <create> marker in the Forms panel and press (Enter). 3. Choose the Quick layout option from the Layout menu.
	Removing a Field	1. While displaying the Forms design screen, choose the Remove field option from the Fields menu. 2. Choose the field you want to remove from the field list.
	Adding and Labeling a Field	1. While displaying the Forms design screen, position the cursor where you want the field text to be positioned, and then type the text. 2. Position the cursor where the field template should be positioned, and then choose the Add field option of the Fields menu. 3. Choose the name of the field to be added.
	Removing and Adding Lines	1. While displaying the Forms design screen, to remove a line, position the cursor on the line you want to remove, and then choose the Remove line option of the Words menu. 2. To add, or insert, a line, position the cursor where the line should be inserted, and then choose the Add line option of the Words menu.
	Adding a Box to a Form	1. While displaying the Forms design screen, choose the Box option of the Layout menu. 2. Choose the single- or double-underline option. 3. Position the cursor where the upper-left corner of the box should be positioned and press (Enter). 4. Use the cursor-movement keys to frame the text, and press (Enter).

Table 4.1	Saving the Form	• To save a form and then remain in the Forms design screen, choose the Save this form option of the Layout menu. Type a name for the form and then press (Enter).
Command Summary (continued)		• To save a form and then exit to the Control Center, choose the Save changes and exit option of the Exit menu. Type a name for the form and then press (Enter).
	Viewing an Existing Form	Highlight the name of the form in the Forms panel, and then press (F2). To return to the Control Center, press (Ctrl)+(End).
	Modifying an Existing Form	Highlight the name of the form in the Forms panel, and then press (Enter). Choose the Modify layout option. To return to the Control Center, press (Ctrl)+(End).
	Creating a Quick Report	1. From the Control Center, highlight the name of a database in the Data panel or the name of a view in the Queries panel.
		2. PRESS: (Shift)+(F9)
		3. To print the report, choose the Begin printing option. To view the report on screen, choose the View report on screen option.
	Changing the Header Band	1. To remove the page number and/or current date from the Header Band, use (Delete) to delete the information.
		2. To change the text for a particular column heading, position the cursor on or near the text to be changed and insert or delete text.

Table 4.1	Changing the Detail Band	To delete the detail information for a particular column, position the cursor in the appropriate field template in the Detail Band and press (Delete) to delete the template. Then delete the column heading.
Command Summary (continued)	Saving a Report	• To save a report and return to the Control Center, choose the Save changes and exit option of the Exit menu. • If you don't want to exit the Reports design screen but want to save your work, choose the Save this report option of the Layout menu.
	Viewing/Printing a Report	• To view the report while designing it, choose the View report on screen option of the Print menu. • To print the report while designing it, choose the Begin printing option of the Print menu. • From the Control Center, highlight the name of the report in the Reports panel and then press (Enter). Then choose the appropriate processing action.
	Modifying a Report	1. Highlight the report filename in the Reports panel of the Control Center and then press (Enter). 2. Choose the Modify layout option.
	Saving a Label Form	1. To save the label form and return to the Control Center, choose the Save changes and exit option of the Exit menu. 2. If you don't want to exit the Labels design screen but want to save your work, choose the Save this label design option of the Layout menu.

Table 4.1	Viewing Labels	1. Highlight the label name in the Labels panel and press (Enter). 2. Choose the Print labels option, and then the View labels on screen option.
Command Summary (concluded)		
	Modifying a Label File	1. Highlight the label name in the Labels panel and press (Enter). 2. Choose the Modify layout option. 3. After making changes to the label form, save the label using the Layout menu or the Exit menu.

KEY TERMS

bands dBASE IV term used to describe the different components of a custom report.

custom report This dBASE IV report format provides greater reporting flexibility than dBASE's quick report format, enabling the user to design all the features to be included in the report. With this command the user can choose the fields to be included in the report and change the descriptive text that appears at the top of each column. Graphic elements can also be added.

form A screen through which you can view and modify the data stored in a database or view.

quick form layout In dBASE IV, this form option provides a simple means for the user to begin creating a form to be used with a database. With this option, every field in the database is included in the form.

quick report dBASE IV reporting option that provides the means to generate a report of the database file or current view; automatically inserts column headings, the current date, and the page number in the report; automatically totals numeric fields. *Compare* custom report.

template When creating forms and labels, a template appears that shows the width and type of each field. For example, an X represents character data and a 9 represents numeric data.

EXERCISES

SHORT ANSWER

1. What is a screen form and why might it be useful to use one?
2. Describe the different components of the custom report screen.
3. What is the difference between the quick report and the custom report?
4. What does the term *bands* refer to, in regard to creating a custom report?
5. What are the different components of a screen form?
6. Describe the procedure for creating mailing labels using dBASE IV.
7. Describe some tasks you can perform when creating a custom report to make the report appear more polished.
8. What is the difference between the header band and the detail band in a report?
9. What is a field template?
10. What is the difference between the column layout and the form layout in a report?

HANDS-ON

1. Using the SUPPLIER database, stored on the Advantage Diskette:
   a. Create a screen form like the one pictured in Figure 4.13.
   b. Save the screen form onto the Advantage Diskette as SUPPLIER.
   c. Using the SUPPLIER form, add two records to the SUPPLIER database.

2. Using the INVOICE database, stored on the Advantage Diskette:
   a. Create a custom report like the one pictured in Figure 4.14.
   b. Save the report onto the Advantage Diskette as INVOICE.
   c. Print the report.

3. Using the SUPPLIER database stored on the Advantage Diskette:
   a. Create mailing labels. *Note*: You may get a message on the screen indicating that there isn't enough space in a given row; you can still view the labels however.
   b. Make two columns of labels print on the page.
   c. Save the labels onto the disk as SUPPLIER.

4. Perform the following steps to practice creating a report:
   a. Set up the EMP-DATA database.
   b. Create the report pictured in Figure 1.5 (in Session 1).
   c. Save the report as EMP-RPT and then print the report.

Figure 4.13

Screen form. This form was created to be used with the SUPPLIER database.

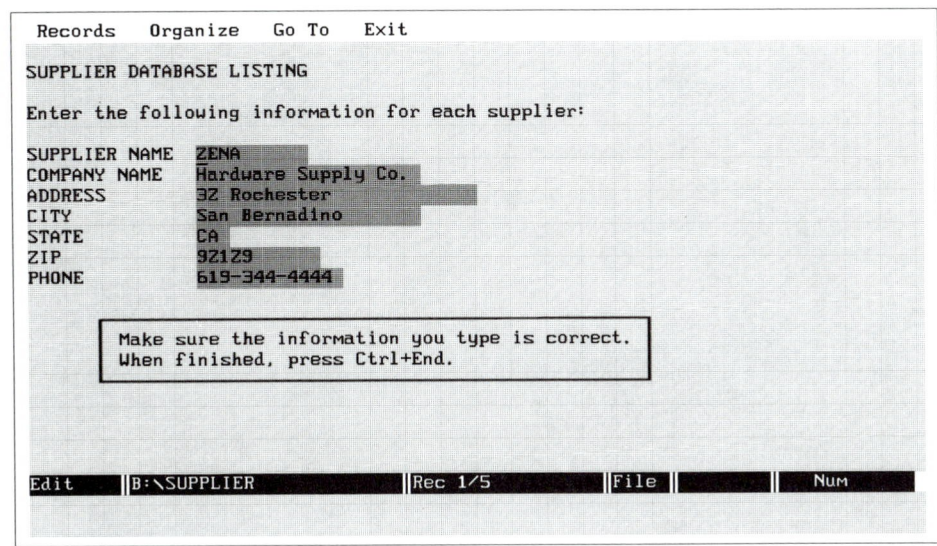

```
 Records    Organize    Go To    Exit

SUPPLIER DATABASE LISTING

Enter the following information for each supplier:

SUPPLIER NAME   ZENA
COMPANY NAME    Hardware Supply Co.
ADDRESS         32 Rochester
CITY            San Bernadino
STATE           CA
ZIP             92129
PHONE           619-344-4444


          ┌──────────────────────────────────────────────┐
          │ Make sure the information you type is correct.│
          │ When finished, press Ctrl+End.                │
          └──────────────────────────────────────────────┘




 Edit      B:\SUPPLIER                    Rec 1/5        File              Num
```

Figure 4.14

Custom report. This report displays data stored in the INVOICE database.

```
Page No.   1
01/14/93

            CUSTOMER INVOICE   ITEM              QUANTITY      UNIT
 INVNUM     NUMBER   DATE      DESCRIPTION        ORDERED       PRICE

 2131       3909     07/14/92  Hammer                   5       2.30
 2132       4809     02/14/92  Nails                   25       0.75
 2133       6211     02/27/92  Broom                    4       8.50
 2140       4999     04/08/92  Broom                    2       8.50
 2138       5100     03/15/92  Mop                     10       5.79
 2136       3906     06/12/92  Screw Driver            11       4.99
 2134       4999     06/12/92  Broom                   18       8.50
 2145       3906     01/04/92  Mop                     14       5.79
                                                       89      45.12




             Cancel viewing: ESC,   Continue viewing: SPACEBAR
```

SESSION 5

MANAGING FILES AND ADVANCED TOPICS

In the last few sessions, you have learned how to create a number of different files with dBASE IV. In this session, you learn how to manage those same files through deleting, copying, moving, and renaming. You will also get a feeling for the depth of dBASE IV's capabilities when we describe some of dBASE's advanced capabilities.

PREVIEW

When you have completed this session, you will be able to:

Display the contents of a different directory.
.
Mark and unmark files.
.
Use dBASE IV to create a database and add data.
.
Delete, copy, move, and rename one or more files.
.
View and edit files.
.
Access DOS directly to perform DOS commands.
.
Create a simple program from the dot prompt.
.
Describe the function of dBASE's Applications Generator.

Why Is This Session Important?
Managing Files
> Displaying Files and Directories
> Marking and Unmarking Files
> Deleting Files
> Moving Files
> Copying Files
> Renaming Files
> Viewing and Editing Files
> Accessing DOS

Simple Program Development
> Accessing the Program Editor

About the dBASE IV Applications
  Generator
Summary
> Command Summary

Key Terms
Exercises
> Short Answer

WHY IS THIS SESSION IMPORTANT?

With the many files that can accumulate on a disk it is important to know how to manage them properly. Otherwise your disk can become cluttered and confused. In this session we lead you through using a number of different file management commands.

In addition, we show you how to create a simple program that can be used to generate mailing labels. We also provide you with an overview of dBASE IV's Applications Generator, which can simplify the process of creating a program, or application.

Before proceeding, make sure the following are true:

1. You have loaded dBASE IV and are displaying the Control Center.

2. Your Advantage Diskette is inserted in the drive. You will save your work onto the diskette and retrieve the files that have been created for you. (*Note*: The Advantage Diskette can be made by copying all the files off the instructor's Master Advantage Diskette onto a formatted diskette.)

3. You have changed the current drive to the one that contains your Advantage Diskette. Remember that dBASE assumes the hard disk is the current drive until you change the drive. Refer to the section on Changing the Current Drive in Session 1 if necessary.

MANAGING FILES

To manage your files, you must access the Tools menu of the Control Center. In the next few sections, we describe the "tools" you need to manage your disk properly, including how to delete, move, copy, and rename files.

Before continuing, we must describe what a subdirectory is. Think of subdirectories as analogous to drawers and folders in a filing cabinet. When storing files on storage devices that are capable of holding large numbers of files, such as a hard disk, the user must be able to put files that pertain to the same category into the same folder, or subdirectory. A **subdirectory**, or **directory**, is a file that contains other files and other subdirectories. Each directory except the root directory is contained in another directory, called its *parent*. The term *directory structure* refers to how a disk is organized into subdirectories.

DISPLAYING FILES AND DIRECTORIES

To list the files stored in the current directory, you must use the DOS utilities option of the Tools menu.

Perform the following steps:

1. Choose DOS utilities option of the Tools menu. The screen should look similar to Figure 5.1. (*Note*: Different files may be displaying on your screen.) Each row of information represents either a subdirectory or a file. A subdirectory is represented with <DIR> in the Size column. The files and subdirectories are listed in alphabetical order. The following describes each column of information that is displaying:

Figure 5.1

Listing files. Using the DOS utilities option of the Tools menu, the files stored on the Advantage Diskette.

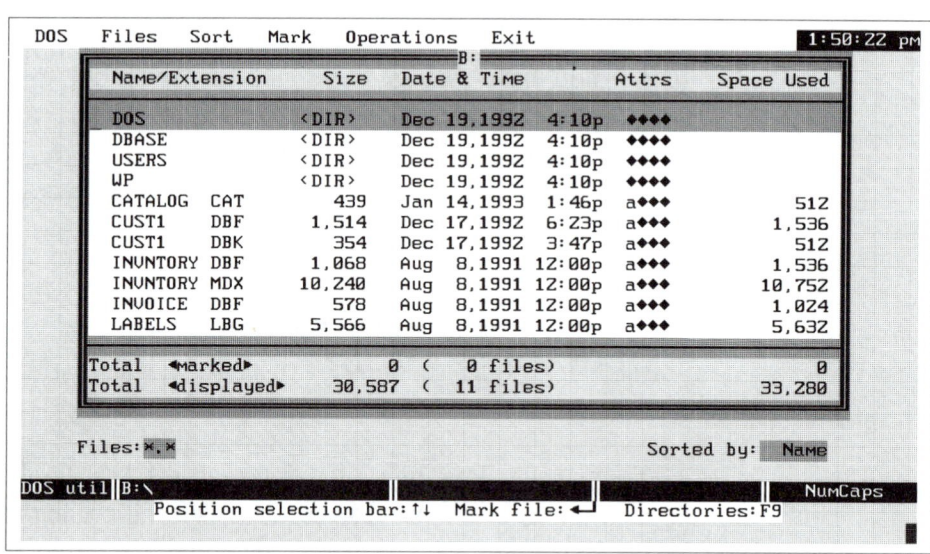

- *Name/Extension*. In this column, the filenames and extensions of the subdirectories and files stored on the current disk are listed.
- *Size*. In this column, <DIR> is listed for all subdirectories. For files, the size of the file (as measured in bytes) is listed.

- *Date & Time*. In this column, the date and time when a subdirectory was created, or when a file was created or last changed, is displayed.
- *Attrs*. This column shows whether an attribute has been set for a file. If no attribute has been set, a small diamond will display in the column. For more information on DOS attributes, refer to a DOS manual.
- *Space Used*. This column shows the space needed on your disk to store the file. This number will always be equal to or greater than the file size, because it depends on the size of the *clusters* your disk uses to store data. For example, if your disk uses a cluster size of 2048 bytes, then even if you store a file that takes up less space, 2048 bytes will still be taken up on the disk.

The two rows on the bottom of the list display summary information relating to all marked files (we describe marking files shortly), as well as all the files stored on the disk.

2. To highlight different files and subdirectories in the list, use ⬆ and ⬇, PgUp and PgDn, or Home and End.

3. To display the contents of a different directory, highlight the directory name and press Enter. A list of the files in that directory will display on the screen. For example, Figure 5.2 shows the screen display for the WP directory on the Advantage Diskette. To display the contents of the directory one level higher in the directory structure, highlight the <parent> marker and press Enter.

Figure 5.2

Listing the files in the WP subdirectory. To list the contents of a subdirectory, highlight the directory name and press Enter.

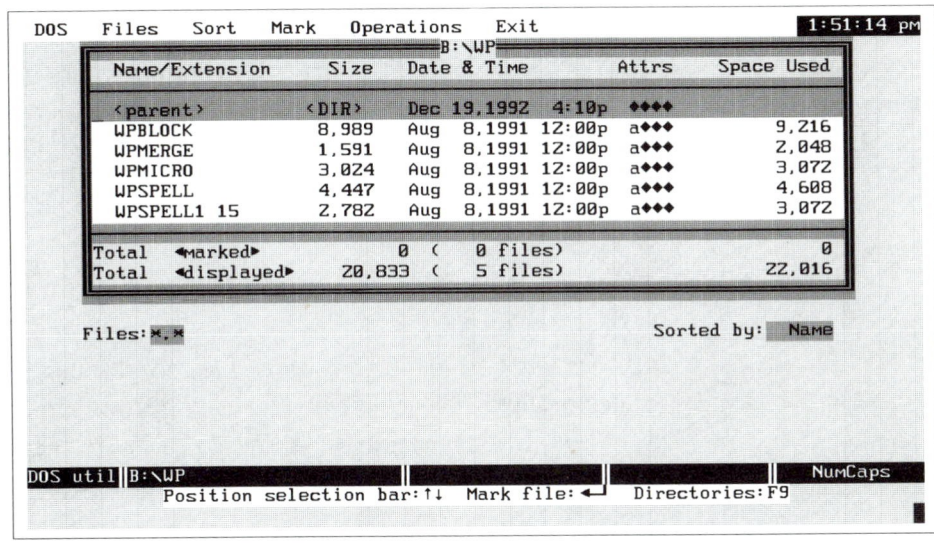

4. To display all the subdirectories stored on a disk, use [F9] (Directories), as indicated on the bottom of the screen. After you press [F9], the screen will look similar to Figure 5.3.

Figure 5.3

Displaying sub-directories. Use [F9] to display all the subdirectories on the current disk.

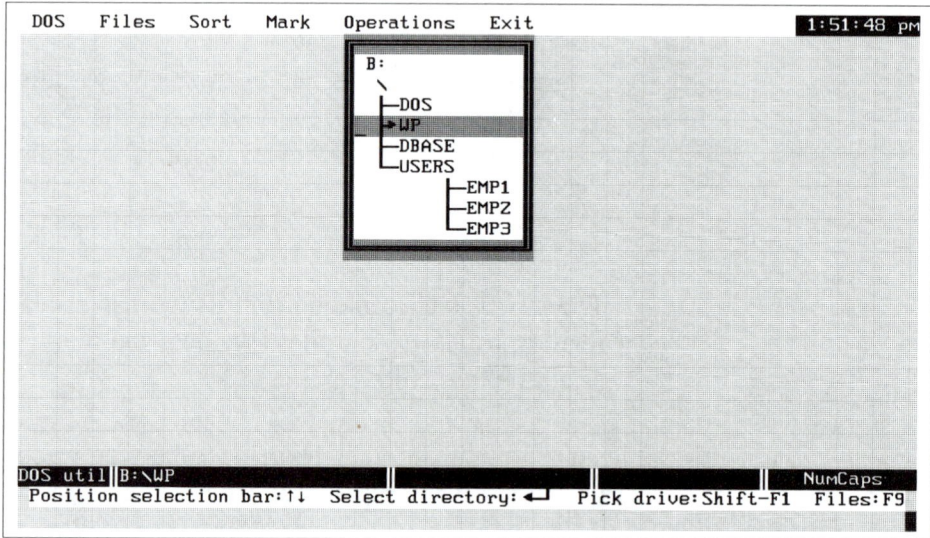

To make a different directory the current directory, highlight it and press [Enter]. A list of the files and subdirectories stored in the current directory will display on the screen.

Quick Reference
Displaying the
Contents of a
Different
Directory

1. Choose the DOS utilities option of the Tools menu.
2. To display the files stored in a directory, highlight the directory name and press [Enter].
3. To see a list of all the subdirectories on a disk, press [F9]. To display the contents of a particular directory, highlight it, and then press [Enter].

MARKING AND UNMARKING FILES

dBASE lets you mark a group of files so you can later erase, copy, move, or delete them. This capability saves you from having to work with one file at a time. In this section we show you how to mark files; in the next few sections we show you how to delete, move, copy, and rename a marked group of files.

To mark a file, highlight the file and press ⟨Enter⟩. An arrow will appear to the left of the filename. The file will remain marked until you exit to the Control Center or access DOS (described shortly). To unmark the same file, press ⟨Enter⟩ while highlighting the filename.

To mark all files in the current directory, choose the Mark all option of the Mark menu. Arrows will appear next to every file in the list (Figure 5.4). To unmark all files in the current directory, choose the Unmark all option of the Mark menu. The Reverse marks option of the Mark menu will unmark all marked files, and mark all unmarked files.

Figure 5.4

Marking files

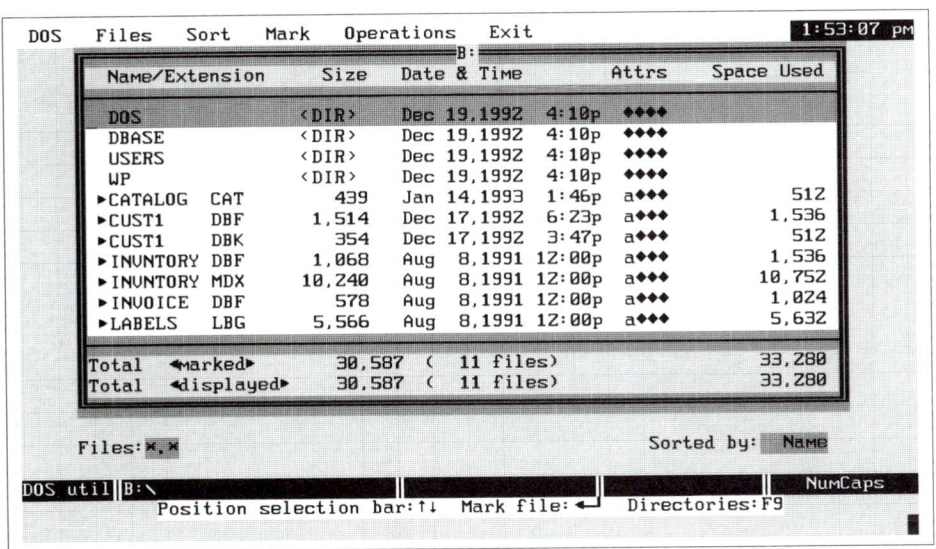

1. To mark an unmarked file, highlight the file and press ⟨Enter⟩.
2. To unmark a marked file, highlight the file and press ⟨Enter⟩.

DELETING FILES

The Operations menu (Figure 5.5) enables you to perform a number of DOS commands without having to access DOS directly. One of the options in the Operations menu is Delete. Instead of taking up disk space by keeping files on disk that you no longer use and don't intend to use in the future, erase the file.

Figure 5.5

The Operations
menu

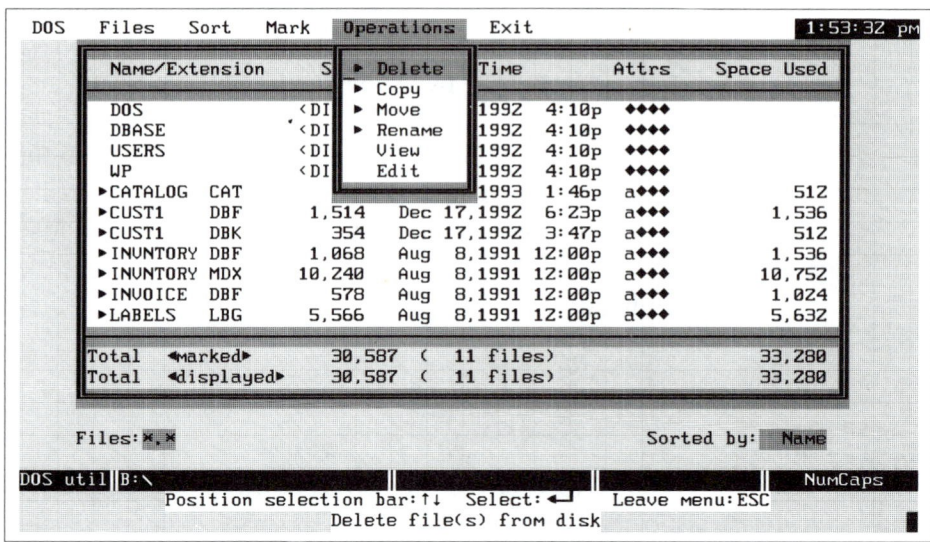

When you choose the Delete option of the Operations menu, dBASE will
ask if you want to delete a single file, the marked files, or all the displayed
files. If you choose the Single File option, dBASE will delete the currently
highlighted file. You can also delete an individual file by highlighting it and
pressing **Delete**.

Quick Reference   1. Choose the Delete option of the Operations menu.
Deleting One   2. Choose the Single File, Marked Files, or Displayed Files option.
or More Files

MOVING FILES

Use the Move option of the Operations menu to move one or more files to
another disk or directory. Once you choose the Move option, dBASE will
ask if you want to move a single file, the marked files, or all the displayed
files. If you choose the Single File option, dBASE will move the currently
highlighted file.

Once you've chosen the files to be moved, dBASE will pause for you to
type the drive or directory to which the files should be moved. In Figure
.5.6, dBASE is waiting for you to specify where the CUST1.DBF file
should be moved. After typing in the target drive or directory, press

(Ctrl)+(End) to execute the command. Press (Esc) to abort, or cancel, the command.

Figure 5.6

Moving a file

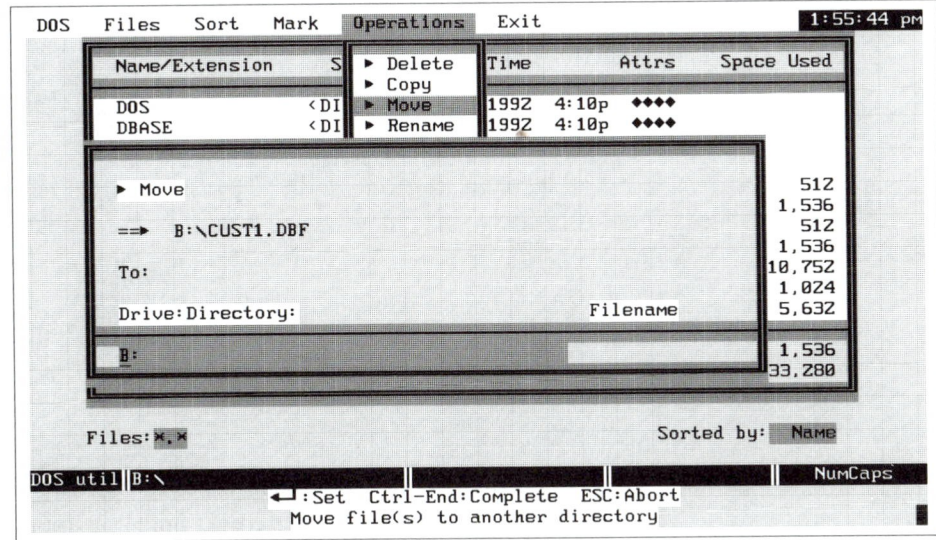

....

Quick Reference
Moving One
or More Files

1. Choose the Move option of the Operations menu.
2. Choose the Single File, Marked Files, or Displayed Files option.
3. Type the drive or directory to which the files should be moved.
4. Press (Ctrl)+(End) to move the files.

....

COPYING FILES

Use the Copy option of the Operations menu to copy one or more files to another disk or directory. Once you choose the Copy option, dBASE will ask if you want to copy a single file, the marked files, or all the displayed files. If you choose the Single File option, dBASE will copy the currently highlighted file.

Once you've chosen the files to be copied, dBASE will pause for you to type the drive or directory to which the files should be copied. After typing in the target drive or directory, press (Ctrl)+(End) to execute the command. Press (Esc) to abort, or cancel, the command.

Quick Reference
Copying One
or More Files

1. Choose the Copy option of the Operations menu.
2. Choose the Single File, Marked Files, or Displayed Files option.
3. Type the drive or directory to which the files should be copied.
4. Press Ctrl + End to move the files.

RENAMING FILES

Use the Rename option of the Operations menu to rename one or more files. dBASE won't let you use a name that already exists in the current directory. Once you choose the Rename option, dBASE will ask if you want to rename a single file, the marked files, or all the displayed files. If you choose the Single File option, dBASE will rename the currently highlighted file.

Once you've chosen the files to be renamed, dBASE will pause for you to type in the new name(s). To rename more than one file at once, the files to be renamed must have similar names, and you must use * to perform the command. For example, suppose you have REPORT.JAN and REPORT.FEB stored on your disk. If you enter the new filename as BUDGET.*, the files will be renamed BUDGET.JAN and BUDGET.FEB.

Quick Reference
Renaming
a File

1. Choose the Rename option of the Operations menu.
2. Choose the Single File, Marked Files, or Displayed Files option.
3. Type the new name, and then press Enter.

VIEWING AND EDITING FILES

The View option of the Operations menu is used to view the contents of, or take a "peek" into, a highlighted file on the screen. This command is useful when you can't remember what file you want to work with. If the displayed file can't fit on the screen, you will be prompted to press the Space Bar to view the rest of the file. If the file you're viewing isn't an ASCII ("clean" text) text file, dBASE will try to filter out any characters that it doesn't understand.

The Edit option of the Operations menu enables you to edit program files (we describe programming shortly), ASCII text files, and files that contain dBASE IV code, such as files with the extension of FMT, FRG, and PRS.

This command shouldn't be used with a dBASE IV database file (a file with the extension of DBF) or with files that have the extension of EXE or COM.

Highlight the file that you want to view, and then choose the View option of the Operations menu.

ACCESSING DOS

By accessing DOS directly you not only have access to many of the commands described in this session (such as delete, copy, and rename), but to all of DOS's commands. For example, you can format a disk using the FORMAT command or use the CHKDSK command to check the status of RAM and of your disks.

To access DOS directly, choose the "Perform DOS command" option of the DOS menu. dBASE will display a prompt box on the screen (Figure 5.7). Type a DOS command into the prompt box and press (Enter). The output of the command will display on the screen. To display the Tools screen, press any key.

Figure 5.7

Accessing DOS.
By accessing
DOS directly, you
can use almost
any of DOS's
commands.

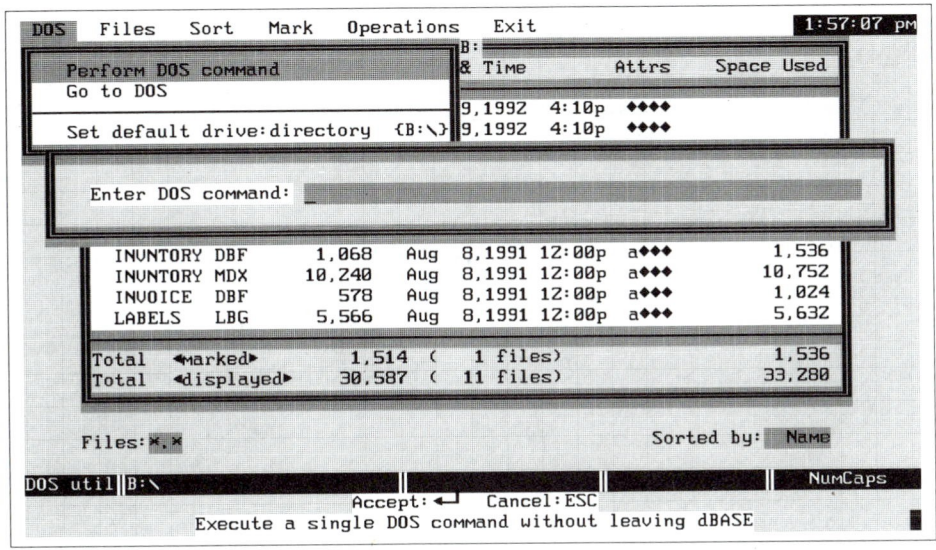

Quick Reference   Choose the Perform DOS command option of the DOS menu.
Accessing DOS

SIMPLE PROGRAM DEVELOPMENT

In this section, we lead you through creating a simple program using dBASE IV. A **program** is a disk file that contains a series of dBASE IV commands. Once you've created a program, you must use, or run, it to realize its benefits. The most common reasons for using command files are to automate procedures that you perform often, thus saving time, and to simplify your interaction with dBASE IV.

Following are the basic steps for developing a program using dBASE IV:

1. Creating the program from the dot prompt using the MODIFY COMMAND command. (*Note*: Later in this session, we describe creating a program using dBASE IV's Application Generator.)

2. Running the program from the dot prompt using the DO command.

3. After running the program, correcting any errors in it.

In this section you will create a program named DOLABEL that will use the CUST1 database and a label file named LABELS, both stored on the Advantage Diskette, to generate mailing labels. We have listed in Table 5.1 each of the command lines that you will enter into the program, and the purpose for each command line.

ACCESSING THE PROGRAM EDITOR

In this section, we lead you through creating a program file named DOLABEL that automates the process of displaying mailing labels on the screen.

Perform the following steps:

1. To display the dot prompt, choose the Exit to dot prompt option of the Exit menu.

2. To initiate the MODIFY COMMAND command and type a name for the program you are creating:
   TYPE: `modify command DOLABEL`
   PRESS: `Enter`
   The screen should look like Figure 5.8.

Table 5.1	*Program File Command*	*Purpose*
Program Commands	TEXT	Initiate Text mode. Anything you type on the following lines will display as descriptive text on the screen until the ENDTEXT command is used.
	CUSTOMER LABEL LISTING	This text will display on the screen.
	ENDTEXT	Stop Text mode.
	USE A:CUST1 *or* USE B:CUST1	Set up the CUST1 database for use.
	LABEL FORM A:LABELS *or* LABEL FORM B:LABELS	Retrieve the LABELS file.

Figure 5.8

The Program Editor screen. When creating a program, type in command instructions here.

3. dBASE is waiting for you to type in command lines that you want to include in the DOLABEL program. Type in each of the program file commands (described in Table 5.1) and press (Enter) at the end of each line. When you finish, the screen should look like Figure 5.9.

Figure 5.9

The DOLABEL program instructions

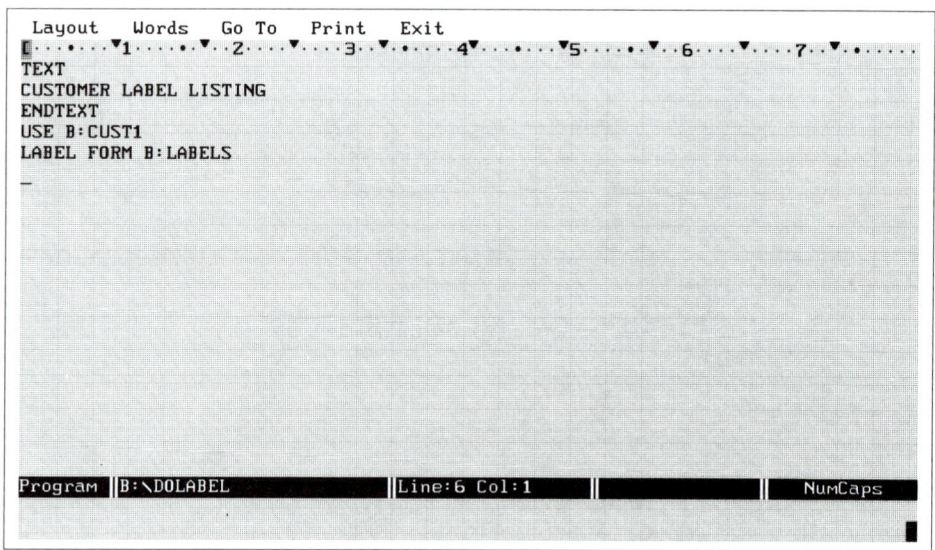

4. Review what you have typed to make sure it is correct. Then, to save the program:
   PRESS: (Ctrl)+(End)
   The dot prompt should again be displaying on the screen.

5. To use the program:
   TYPE: do DOLABEL
   PRESS: (Enter)
   When the program finishes executing, the screen should look similar to Figure 5.10.

6. To edit the program file, simply type modify command followed by the program name and then press (Enter). The program lines will appear on the screen so that you can edit them.

Figure 5.10

After you run the DOLABEL program, customer labels will display on the screen.

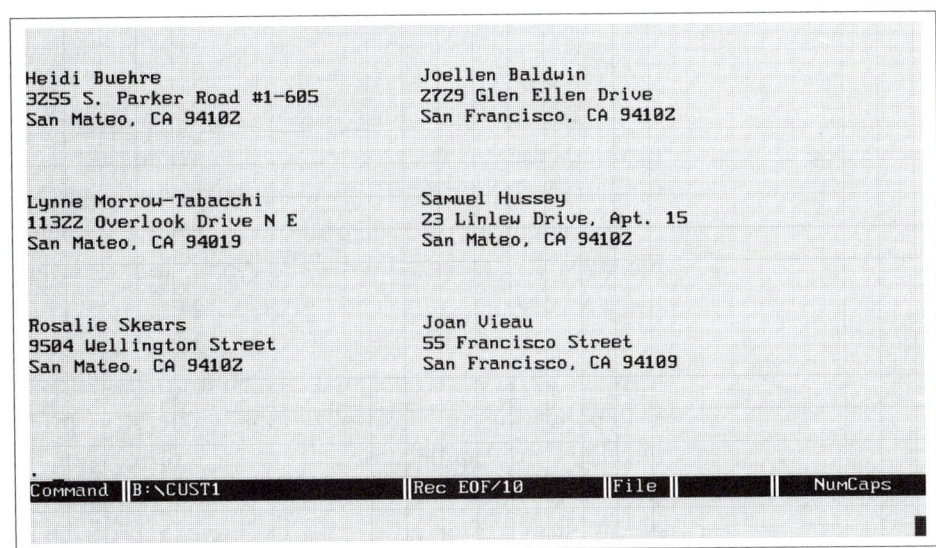

```
Heidi Buehre                      Joellen Baldwin
3255 S. Parker Road #1-605        2729 Glen Ellen Drive
San Mateo, CA 94102               San Francisco, CA 94102


Lynne Morrow-Tabacchi             Samuel Hussey
11322 Overlook Drive N E          23 Linlew Drive, Apt. 15
San Mateo, CA 94019               San Mateo, CA 94102



Rosalie Skears                    Joan Vieau
9504 Wellington Street            55 Francisco Street
San Mateo, CA 94102               San Francisco, CA 94109




Command ‖B:\CUST1             ‖Rec EOF/10       ‖File ‖        ‖   NumCaps
```

Quick Reference
To Create and Save a Program

1. While viewing the Control Center, choose the Exit to dot prompt option from the Exit menu.
2. TYPE: MODIFY COMMAND *program name*
3. PRESS: [Enter]
4. Type the commands you want to enter into the program.
5. To save the program:
   PRESS: [Ctrl]+[End]

Quick Reference
Using a Program

After the dot prompt:
TYPE: DO *program name*
PRESS: [Enter]

Quick Reference
Modifying a Program

1. After the dot prompt:
   TYPE: MODIFY COMMAND *program name*
   PRESS: [Enter]
2. Your program will appear on the screen.
3. After making changes, to save the program:
   PRESS: [Ctrl]+[End]

ABOUT THE dBASE IV APPLICATIONS GENERATOR

In the last section, you wrote a short program that enables you to create mailing labels. In this section we would like to introduce you to the fundamentals of dBASE IV's Applications Generator. The objective of this section isn't for you to learn how to use the Applications Generator; rather we want you to know what the Applications Generator is and what some of its capabilities are. The dBASE IV **Applications Generator** is a component of dBASE IV that helps you to create programs, or **applications**, which means that you don't have to write a program to build an application. The Applications Generator provides an easy way to develop an application if your processing needs are relatively straightforward. For example, suppose you are the owner of a sporting goods store. You have just begun using dBASE IV to keep track of customer information. You are currently using the following files:

    a.   A customer database named CUSTOMER.DBF
    b.   A screen form for the database named CUST.SCR
    c.   A report named CUST.FRM

Your employees haven't had any training using the dBASE IV Control Center and you don't have time to familiarize them with it. You need an application that will simplify for your employees the process of entering customer information and generating a report. Specifically, you need an application that will display a menu similar to the following and from which your employees can choose the appropriate processing option:

    MAIN PROCESSING MENU
    Choose one of the following options:
    1.   Add a customer record
    2.   Change/delete a customer record
    3.   View a customer report

With dBASE IV's Applications Generator, you can easily create such a menu system; without the Applications Generator, you will need to know much more about programming with dBASE IV. The Applications Generator refers to the components of an application as **objects**. For example, the CUSTOMER.DBF, CUST.SCR, and CUST.FRM files are all considered objects; these particular objects are considered non-Applications Generator objects and are created using the Control Center. The objects you create with the Applications Generator are the menus that display, and the corresponding processes that should be performed when a menu option is chosen. In other words, the Applications Generator creates the dBASE code to tie the different objects together that you need to use in your application.

Following are the basic steps for creating an application with the Applications Generator and then using the application:

1. Decide what you want the application to do for you. For example, do you want employees to be able to edit data in the customer database? Generate a report? Do you want them to view the database through a special screen form?

2. Using the Control Center, create any database, screen form, report form, or index files that your application will need to use.

3. Load the Applications Generator from the Control Center by choosing the <create> marker of the Applications panel. Once it is loaded, the screen will look like Figure 5.11. To begin you must type a name for the application and the name of the database you want to use. When finished, press [Ctrl]+[End].

Figure 5.11

Creating an application using the Applications Generator

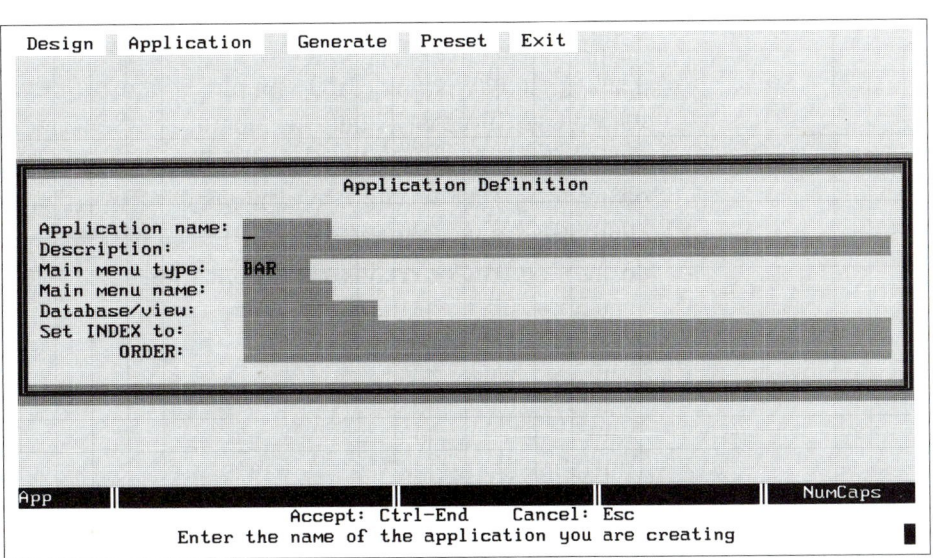

4. Using the Applications Generator, create a menu and then assign processing tasks to each menu option. When finished, save the application onto the disk. The application will be given the extension of APP.

5. Once it's created, to run an application, you highlight the name of the application in the Applications panel, press (Enter), and choose the Run application option. (Or, to modify the application, choose the Modify application option.)

SUMMARY

After using dBASE for even a short period of time, you will begin to accumulate a large number of files. It is important to know how to manage these files. The Tools menu, accessed from the Control Center, provides a number of disk and file management commands. dBASE enables you to work with one file at a time or mark a group of files that you later erase, copy, or move.

A program is a disk file that contains a series of dBASE IV commands. A program is intended to save you time and to simplify your interaction with dBASE IV. To create a program, first display the dot prompt and then use the MODIFY COMMAND command. After typing the program, save the program by pressing (Ctrl)+(End).

The Applications Generator simplifies the process of creating a program with dBASE IV. The Applications Generator views the different components of an application as objects and enables you to tie different objects together with a useful menu system. If your processing needs are straightforward, the Applications Generator provides an easy and convenient way of creating an application.

COMMAND SUMMARY

The table on the following pages provides a list of the commands and procedures covered in this session.

Table 5.2 Command Summary	Displaying the Contents of a Different Directory	1. Choose the DOS utilities option of the Tools menu. 2. To display the files stored in a directory, highlight the directory name and press [Enter]. 3. To see a list of all the subdirectories on a disk, press [F9]. To display the contents of a particular directory, highlight it, and then press [Enter].
	Marking and Unmarking a File	1. To mark an unmarked file, highlight the file and press [Enter]. 2. To unmark a marked file, highlight the file and press [Enter].
	Deleting One or More Files	1. Choose the Delete option of the Operations menu. 2. Choose the Single File, Marked Files, or Displayed Files option.
	Moving One or More Files	1. Choose the Move option of the Operations menu. 2. Choose the Single File, Marked Files, or Displayed Files option. 3. Type the drive or directory to which the files should be moved. 4. Press [Ctrl]+[End] to move the files.
	Copying One or More Files	1. Choose the Copy option of the Operations menu. 2. Choose the Single File, Marked Files, or Displayed Files option. 3. Type the drive or directory to which the files should be copied. 4. Press [Ctrl]+[End] to move the files.
	Renaming a File	1. Choose the Rename option of the Operations menu. 2. Choose the Single File, Marked Files, or Displayed Files option. 3. Type the new name and press [Enter].

Table 5.2 Command Summary (concluded)	Viewing a File	Highlight the file that you want to view, and then choose the View option of the Operations menu.
	Accessing DOS	Choose the Perform DOS command option of the DOS menu.
	To Create and Save a Simple Program	1. While viewing the Control Center, choose the Exit to dot prompt option from the Exit menu. 2. TYPE: MODIFY COMMAND *program name* 3. PRESS: [Enter] 4. Type the commands you want to enter into the program. 5. To save the program, press [Ctrl]+[End]
	Using a Program	After the dot prompt: TYPE: DO *program name* PRESS: [Enter]
	Modifying a Program	1. After the dot prompt: TYPE: MODIFY COMMAND *program name* PRESS: [Enter] 2. Your program will appear on the screen. 3. After making changes, to save the program, press [Ctrl]+[End]

KEY TERMS

applications   Software programs.

applications generator   Software system that generates computer programs in response to the user's needs. The system consists of precoded modules that perform various functions. The user selects the functions he or she needs, and the applications generator determines how to perform the tasks and produces the necessary instructions for the software program.

directory   A file, or subdirectory, that contains other fields and other subdirectories. Subdirectories are analogous to drawers and folders in a filing cabinet.

objects   The dBASE IV Applications Generator refers to different components of an application as *objects.*

program   Group of related instructions that perform specific processing tasks.

subdirectory   A file, or directory, that contains other files and other subdirectories. Subdirectories are analogous to drawers and folders in a filing cabinet.

EXERCISES

SHORT ANSWER

1. What is the function of dBASE IV's Applications Generator?
2. What is the procedure for marking and unmarking a file?
3. Why might you want to access DOS directly when using dBASE IV?
4. What would the procedure be to delete all the files displaying in the current subdirectory?
5. What would the procedure be to copy all the files stored on a disk onto a different disk?
6. From the dot prompt, what command is used to create a program?
7. To execute a program from the dot prompt, what command must you use?
8. When might you want to view the contents of a file on the screen?
9. Why is it a good idea to delete files you no longer need?
10. What would the procedure be to move all the files stored on a disk onto a different disk?